Y0-DOL-560

CRIME FIGHTERS' PSYCHOLOGY:

- Critical Thinking
- Common Sense
  and
- Urban Survival

Bernd W. Weiss, Ph.D.
Hilda O. Weiss, M.B.A.

Copyright © 2000 by Hiles and Hardin Publishers. All rights reserved. No part of this book may be reproduced in any form or by any means, electronic or mechanical, including information storage and retrieval systems, without permission in writing from the publisher.

First Printing

Published by
Hiles and Hardin Publishers
P.O. Box 8692
Calabasas, California 91302-8692
Ph. (818) 883-6610.

Library of Congress
Catalog Card Number: 97-70802
ISBN: 0-931373-04-2

Printed in the United States of America

Dedication

We are dedicating this book to ATAMA (Ameri can Teachers Association of the Martial Arts), ISOK (International Society of Okinawan/Japanese Karate-Do), ITKF (International Traditional Karate Federation) and WFKO (World Federation of Karate-Do Organizations). These are major organizations of and for legitimate martial arts practitioners devoted to human development and self-defense.

This book is also dedicated to the following people in Australia, a country of great potential and the uniform of which Bernie wore with pride at Singleton's Lone Pine Barracks and in Sydney:

Mary and Michael Angel, Clifton Gardens
Robyn and Ron Borg, Toongabbie
Barry and Andrew Bradshaw, Melbourne
Patti Chomentowski, Randwick
Ian Froggatt, Ballina
Dick and Margret Dicalfas, Maroubra
Br. Frank M. Harding (Posthumous), Paddington
Peter and Beverly Klasups, Wagga Wagga
Michael Leahy, Killara
Ted and Joan Leahy, Tabulam
Eileen and Murray Johnson, Parkes
Ian Pollet, Orange
Herbert, Robyn and Luke Samitz, Hurstville
David Vaughan, Singleton
Frank, Luise and Orana Wyss, Canberra

Very Special Supporters

Mr. Donald Buck, Judan, Kyokushin Karate

Mr. Edwin Hamile, Kudan, Shotokan Karate

Dr. Duke Moore, Judan, Karate, Judo, Ju Jitsu

Mr. Shoshin Nagamine, Judan, Shorin Ryu Karate

Mr. Hidetaka Nishiyama, Kudan, Shotokan Karate

Posthumous Honorees

Mr. William Langridges, Sandan, Shotokan Karate
(Pioneering Karate Teacher in Sydney, Australia)
Mr. John Pereira, Hachidan, Wado Ki Kai Karate
Dr. Frank Puskas, Judan, Shotokan Karate, Ju Jitsu
Dr. Alexander Vilumsons, Hachidan, Shotokan Ka-
rate, Ju Jitsu and Kung Fu

Table of Contents

iv

Photographs

v

Acknowledgments

Langridges Gym and the Woolloomooloo Police Boy's Club both in Sydney, Australia gave Bernd Weiss his first formal start in the martial arts as of 1955. ATAMA's (American Teachers Association of the Martial Arts) Dr. Duke Moore, the late Mr. John Pereira, Mr. Jery Streeter, and many other outstanding self-defense experts, are strong influences we should thank for encouragement and information with respect to this book.

Cofounder of ISOK (International Society of Okinawan/Japanese Karate-Do), Leroy Rodrigues has been and is continuing to be a positive influence on us. We should also mention the West Los Angeles Karate School with which we were connected for many years. There also is Shihan Edwin Hamile of WFKO (World Federation of Karate-Do Organizations), Mr. Tak Kubota of the IKA (International Karate Association), Mr. Barry Bradshaw of the AAMAA (Australian-American Martial Arts Alliance), Don & Fred Buck of the AKA (American Kyokushin Association) and Mr. Hidetaka Nishiyama of the ITKF (International Traditional Karate Federation).

Ms. Phyllis Keeney of L.A. Southwest College, Mr. Mike Gerber of L.A. Pierce College, Sgt. Virginia Hawkins (ret.) and Sgt. Pitkin of the L.A. County Sheriff Dept. also helped by providing valuable information contained in this book.

Our thanks are also extended to our colleagues at the Los Angeles Police Department who helped with the development of self-defense applications. We are particularly grateful to the excellent training staff at the LAPD academy. Sgt. Bob Kellar and Sgt. Conta provided outstanding leadership for the training of us recruits. They were augmented by such quality police officers as Ofcr. Judy Cortland, Ofcr. Sandy Hazlewood, Ofcr. Mike Henley, Ofcr. Jim Katapodis, Ofcr. James Lew, Ofcr. Jerry Mulford, Ofcr. Annette Olivas, Ofcr. Jorge Padilla, Ofcr. Ken Santolla, Ofcr. Mike Schwehr, and Ofcr. Pete Valdez whose inputs enriched our ideas regarding the contents of this book.

As professionals in higher/adult education we must compliment the staff (both leadership and rank and file) of the LAPD Academy. Although virtually all of them are police officers and not professional educators, through intelligence and dedication, they have developed an academy, which has training and education programs that are so sophisticated they can serve as models for many university and college administrators and professors.

Gratitude compels us to mention the great New South Wales Police Force in Australia under whose auspices the Woolloomooloo Police Boys Club gave Bernie his initial exposure to fighting arts when he was 12 years old. He also received his first karate training at Langridges's Gym in Sydney where he earned his first black belt in 1958.

We would also like to thank the dedicated Police Officers with whom we have had the pleasure of working LAPD's West Valley Area. We should give special mention to Ofcr. Dave Buck, Ofcr. Lou Merritt, Ofcr. Esta Yonce (ret.), Ofcr. Tony Newsom, Ofcr. "Oley" Olson and many more. The following officers also deserve our gratitude:

Aguilar	La Grassa	Monroe
Allan	Lane	Norton
Andert	Lantiser	Pryor
Baker	Lemmonds	Rose
Ballard	Li	Rosenfeld
Beatty	Little	Rudolph
Becker	Long	Serna
Boen	Longobardi	Sodoma
Chupala	Love	Solter
Cox	Madigan	Stark
De Miglio	Mathews	Tisdale
Eicher	McCloud	Toth
Guittierez	McCoy	Webb
Harrison	McElroy	Williams
Howe	McNemara	Williamson
Kane	Miller	Zwinger
Kempner	Mitchel	Zvi

The numerous survivors of vicious attacks who shared their experiences with us also deserve praise. These include the nine year old girl who successfully foiled a kidnap attempt as well as the six foot adult, male who was set upon by four attackers in a parking lot. Between these two extremes in size and weight, we interviewed many victims whose stories enhanced the strategies and tactics of urban survival.

We also owe our thanks to the Topanga-Valley Karate School students who volunteered to be the models for the photographs in this book. They include the following:

Marcine Bitner	Patrick Doherty
Jake Gularian	Cory Holdstock
Warren Hull	Steve Langa
Bob Logan	Duke Moore
Richard Preble	Claire Thorne
Emily Thorne	Ginger Weston

Special thanks are owed to the late Dr. Frank Puskas for his insights into, and field research on, crime prevention and self-defense.

Preface

This book is an outgrowth of three sets of experiences: Martial arts/self-defense instruction, previous publications and police experience.

Between the two of us, we total nearly 70 years of martial arts training and teaching which includes judo, jujitsu, kobu-jitsu, Western boxing and firearms training and several systems of karate. The primary unarmed fighting system that we practice and advocate is shotokan karate. For over 20 years Bernie has taught self-defense and karate at L.A. Southwest College, Pierce College, UCLA, WLA Karate School, Learning Tree University and for the Los Angeles Police Department. Hilda has taught and co-taught self-defense classes for UCLA, Pierce College, Learning Tree University and LAPD.

We co-founded and teach at the nonprofit Topanga-Valley Karate School which we started in 1975. Of the thousands of students that we've taught over the years, less than 30 have been seriously attacked. The others have avoided danger. Furthermore, all of the intended "victims" were able to successfully fight off their attackers using the knowledge they gained from us.

Our publications include magazines and newspaper articles as well as books. Beginning in 1976 we wrote a series of articles for newspapers as well as martial arts magazines. Also since 1976 we have co-edited **Karate Profile** a technical martial arts magazine for experts in the field. Currently Bernie is a regular contributor to **Bugeisha Magazine** and the German language **Tamashi Magazin**.

Bernie's 1977 book, **Woman As Victim** was published as a non-commercial, educational booklet which turned out to be a "best seller." In 1986 Bernie co-authored with the late Dr. Frank Puskas, **Psychology and Methods of Survival** which was used by self-defense instructors all over the world. Hilda and Bernie co-authored the 1992 book **Self-defense For Everybody: A Primer in Applied Karate**. This book is currently a very popular item on every continent. Hilda has also written articles for **Black Belt Magazine, Karate Illustrated** and **Karate Profile**. Urban Survival replaced, updated and expanded upon, the **Psychology and Methods of Survival** book. This book, in turn, does the same with the **Urban Survival** book.

Much of our crime knowledge comes from being reserve police officers with the Los Angeles Police Department (LAPD). Bernie is an unpaid, uniformed, part-time police officer whose, at times dangerous, street assignments bring him into contact with both victims and criminals on a regular basis. For many years he has worked patrol units responding to '911' calls and currently is working in the Fugitive Warrant Section. Hilda is also an unpaid volunteer working as a crime prevention and self-defense specialist.

We begin this book with the telephone because it is often abused by burglars, rapists, child molesters, etc., in order to get information about potential victims. We cover rape early in the book because it is the fastest growing violent crime in America and devote two chapters to this particular crime. Prevention and confrontation is then the subject of Chapter #4.

As violence in America continues to dramatically increase (e.g., there is a murder every 21 seconds) fighting, both armed and unarmed, and learning to fight are becoming increasingly more important. We have therefore devoted four chapters to this topic.

Safety on the road and home security are also areas of concern for those interested in urban survival. We consequently included these in Chapter #9 and Chapter #10.

People are family oriented which makes child safety and domestic violence important. Two chapters (11 and 12) are about these topics.

In this book we are introducing Bernie Weiss' theory on using taste to predict, and avoid, danger (Chapter 13).

In Chapter 14 we are also adding Hilda's research on the body language cues which are often used by perpetrators to choose their victims. These same cues can also be used by potential victims to avoid attacks.

As Americans we pride ourselves on being part of a society of equitable laws which are fairly administered. Unfortunately this is not necessarily true. In fact, the victim is all too often victimized by the legal system after being physically or emotionally injured by an attacker. To provide fuller information about this aspect of urban survival, we included a chapter on the legal system.

In our final chapter we summarize easy to use—and to remember—aspects of urban survival.

You can begin reading with any chapter, however we encourage you to read the whole book because much of the material is interrelated. A thorough reading will give you the best understanding of how to optimize your own survival and success.

The Telephone

The Obscene Phone Call

Women in particular are consistently the targets of certain crimes such as obscene phone calls, mashings, purse- snatchings, rapes, etc. According to a General Telephone spokesperson a little over 85% of people who receive obscene phone calls are women. This chapter is about the actions a woman (or anyone) can take in response to such nuisance calls. Later chapters will inform and advise readers about other crimes.

Telephone companies categorize <u>nuisance</u>, or <u>annoyance</u>, calls into several types, and the obscene phone call is one type. Other types include solicitation calls (sales or appeals for donations), harassing creditors' or debt collectors' calls, wrong numbers, etc.

It is the obscene phone call, however, that seems to be the most disconcerting type of call for many people. Parents tend to be concerned about their children listening to obscenities, and many women are concerned about the obscene caller following up with personal confrontations.

The most common advice given to victims of such calls is to remain calm and to simply hang up.

General Telephone's Phillip Sheridan suggests, "the best thing to do is <u>not</u> to react to such a call at all, just hang the phone gently into the cradle." This is generally the most effective response to an obscene phone call.

Such callers want a response from their intended victims. Shock, anger, or talking to the caller provides him with the reactions he thrives on. By gently hanging up the phone the victim <u>deprives</u> the caller of the incentive to make the call—namely, a reaction.

Although gently hanging up the phone is normally good advice and is usually effective, there are some callers who persist regardless of the victim's reaction or non-reaction. Out of the tens of thousands of obscene phone call complaints received each year by the major telephone companies, only about 5%-6% are persistent.

If you are harassed by persistent annoyance calls, keep as detailed a log of these calls as possible. Such a log should contain the following information:

1. *The number and frequency of such calls. Every day, once per week, weekends only, etc.*
2. *The dates and the exact times of day or night these calls are made, and the length of each call.*
3. *Description of the calls. Heaviness of breathing, the actual words spoken, calmness or anger in the caller's voice, etc.*

4. *Notes about accents, speech patterns, or voice pitch (husky or high-pitched, for example).*
5. *Notes about any background noises such as traffic, television or radio, voices of other people or animals, etc.*
6. *Notes about who was or wasn't at home when the phone calls were received.*

Police and telephone company representatives advise victims of persistent nuisance callers to simply change their telephone number. Pacific Bell, for instance, will allow their customers to change their number once a year for free. Approximately half of these victims actually change their numbers which usually stops such calls.

However, for business or other reasons, it is often very difficult for victims to change their telephone number.

If the victim cannot change the number and continues to receive annoyance calls, he or she can report them to the local police or sheriff's department. Different jurisdictions and law enforcement agencies vary somewhat in the way they handle such reports, but the Los Angeles Police Department's procedures are quite typical.

A victim can go to an LAPD station and make a police report to the desk officer. A detective assigned to annoyance calls studies the report and may, under particular circumstances, interview any possible suspects. Usually the phone calls stop after these police interviews. Sometimes, however, they continue. At this point the victim will be advised to call the business office of the local telephone company. A representative of the phone company will then discuss various options with the victim.

If legal and circumstantial conditions warrant it, the phone company can put a "trap" on the line in order to trace where the phone calls originate. Setting up traps does involve personnel and time, consequently they are rarely used unless there is very good cause to believe they will lead to the culprit. Even when used, these traps may not produce results because, for instance, the caller may be calling from different pay phones.

However, sometimes traps do produce results. General Telephone's Phillip Sheridan pointed out, "...some offenders have been caught before they left a coin telephone booth."

New computerized equipment and fiberoptic "lines" allows phone companies to give the customer a list of phone numbers from which phone calls are made to his or her telephone. Furthermore, the precise time and date of each call can also be listed. This would make it considerably cheaper and easier to identify nuisance callers. At the writing of this book, this technology is being installed by telephone companies in many areas. Some telephone companies have a "pound 69" service for a small monthly fee. When you push the pound symbol followed by pressing the 6 and the 9, it will ring the telephone from which the most recent call was made to you. This way you can call a hang-up or annaoyance caller which may help you to identify him/her.

Answering The Telephone

The telephone call is often a convenient tool for potential thieves, rapists, burglars or mashers (men who try to force their attention upon unwilling women without necessarily raping them) to obtain information about their potential or intended victims. The way the intended victim responds to inquiring calls may determine whether he or she will, in fact, be a victim. Revealing that you are at home alone, for example, is providing a rapist or robber with the information he wants. Or, indicating that you are about to go to a movie may be an invitation to be burglarized.

When you answer the telephone, you are not obligated to answer questions, regardless of who the caller claims to be. A caller may, for instance, claim to be a census taker to get information that can be used against you. He or she may also claim to be a part of a market research team in order to obtain information about you. In any case don't answer questions until you get the caller's name and phone number and check authenticity by calling the appropriate authorities or institutions.

Always ask any stranger who calls to identify himself and to give you his number. If you're alone at home, do not reveal that you are in fact alone. Furthermore, if the caller refuses to give you the information you ask of him, simply hang up. If a stranger calls and requests your address, refuse to give it to him or her. The caller may be a rapist or burglar trying to pay you an unwanted visit.

If a salesperson calls you about a product or service you don't want, tell him or her that you are not interested and hang up. Don't let them keep you on the phone—just hang up.

If you are interested in what the salesperson is selling, your safest strategy is to take his name and number as well as the name and number of his firm. Then tell him that you would like to check on him and his firm and that you will call back later. If he is legitimate, he will not object. Don't be taken in by "bargains" which you must purchase now or the price will go up or the stock will run out. Check the salesperson and his firm, which should be listed in the phone book. You can check the firm by contacting the Better Business Bureau. Be careful not to use the phone number the caller gives you until you verify it. Often a con artist will have a person answer the phone pretending to represent the company.

Do not let anyone into your home to use the telephone. Using your phone may be a ploy to gain entrance to your home in order to hurt you, set you up for a later burglary, or both. If you want to help strangers, offer to make the call yourself while they wait outside.

Train your children and instruct your babysitter or other workers around your house to give no information about the family or the house/apartment over the phone.

Answering machines are helpful devices for protecting individuals living alone. A recorded message using a masculine voice can explain that "no one can come to the phone at the moment" and that the caller should give his name and phone number before hanging up. The message should not say or imply that the house is unoccupied or that you are alone. Overly specific messages risk inviting unwanted visitors.

It is advisable, particularly if you live alone, to have a second telephone within the reach of your bed. If someone enters your home while you're in bed, you have access to a phone. A second bedroom telephone should not merely be an extension. A burglar or rapist can stop you from using your extension simply by lifting the receiver off any other phone in the house. For the sake of security, therefore, your bedside telephone should have its own line and unlisted number.

Psychology

As far back as 1957 Leon Festinger described his <u>Cognitive Dissonance</u> theory. He based this theory partly on Kurt Lewin's **Field Theory** and Fritz Heider's **Balance Theory**. According to this theory, we feel uncomfortable when there is disharmony (i.e., dissonance) between different attitudes, beliefs or perceptions that we have. This discomfort motivates us either to avoid potentially dissonant situations or to change our attitudes or behaviors.

The obscene phone caller, for instance, wants a particular response from his or her victim. When he does not get that response—and hears nothing but the click of the receiver being placed into the cradle—Festinger's cognitive dissonance theory predicts that he will feel uncomfortable ("...a negative motivational state") and will be motivated to reduce his dissonance. She or he often does this by not calling the victim again. In fact, <u>most</u> obscene callers don't persist when the victim consistently hangs up.

Sometimes burglars or rapists pretending to be salespersons will attempt to create dissonance in you so that you will give them the information they need to victimize you.

A rapist might try to pass himself off to you as a T.V.

pollster doing a telephone survey of viewing preferences. If you hesitate to answer the questions, you might be told that your answers may help improve the quality of T.V. programming which in turn is good for country, motherhood and apple pie. The caller may imply that if you don't give revealing answers you are somehow a "bad" person. This is designed to create dissonance which you can reduce by cooperating with the caller who may later use the information you give to victimize you.

Chapter 1

Name:_____

Question 1

On the remainder of this page use your own words to briefly describe Cognitive Dissonance Theory.

Chapter 1

Name:_____

Briefly explain how Cognitive Dissonance theory helps to describe criminal abuses of the telephone.

Rape

The Act Of Rape

Rape, the fastest growing violent crime in America, is an act of aggression. Rape is <u>not</u>, as some people claim and believe, an act of sexuality or an act of love. Rather, rape is an assault in which the victim's body is abused. The rapist uses his own body to inflict pain and humiliation upon the victim. Police data show that slightly over half the reported rapes are anal, oral, or both. The remainder, slightly less than half, are vaginal.

The rape victim may be knocked unconscious, beaten into submission, or threatened at gun or knife point. Often the assault is brutal and the threat of death is used to force compliance. The victim is too terrified to relate to any sexual aspect of the rape.

The *California Law Review* states that 85% of reported rapes involved at least some force by the rapist. Twenty percent of the victims were brutally beaten. However, murder is a rare concomitant of sexual assaults.

Surprise is on the rapist's side. By the time the victim becomes aware of the terrible situation that the rapist has imposed upon her, she has often been rendered mentally or physically powerless. The victim's lack of power together with her terror, humiliation and embarrassment makes the rape a horrifying experience—an experience that is aggravated by the physical insults to her body.

In the light of this horror, pain, and fear which are integral parts of the rape act, it is surprising that some people still cling to such myths as the victim "must have asked for it," or that she "enjoyed it." Instead, interviews and surveys consistently show that rape victims experience tremendous emotional and physical trauma, through no fault of their own, at the hands of their attacker.

Since rape is <u>forced</u> upon the victim, <u>consent</u> is not even a plausible issue. Yet many people still believe the old myth that rape is impossible without consent.

Although most of the reported rapes occur at night, a sufficient number occur throughout the day to render no time slot particularly safe. According to Dr. Amir, a noted behavioral scientist, and others, over one-third involve rapists who have forced their way into the victims' homes, and over half the rapes are committed inside residences. Frequently the rapist knows the victim. In fact, date rape, where the victim is raped by a man who has invited her out, is increasing particularly fast. Overall, about 80% of the rapists know the victim at least on a first name basis.

Most rapes are not done on impulse. Dr. Amir's study of over 600 rapes revealed that over 90% of the group or gang rapes, 83% of the pair rapes (two rapists attacking one woman), and 58% of the single rapes were planned. Furthermore, much of the planning done by the rapist was detailed and elaborate, often without any particular victim in mind. The victim happened to be unfortunate enough to be randomly chosen.

Dr. J. Selkin, a psychologist who has studied rapists, cites data showing that most rapists seek vulnerable victims. Examples of particularly vulnerable victims include women or children who are intoxicated by alcohol and other drugs, are sleeping, or are very young or very old. Women living alone or living in easily entered residences are also prey for the rapist.

There is also evidence based on surveys and data comparing police statistics with those of rape crisis hotlines and clinics, that most rapes are not reported. That is to say, the total number of actual rapes far exceeds the number reported to police agencies. During a recent 12-month period over 80,000 rapes were reported in the U.S. Yet educated estimates place the actual total number somewhere between 2 and 10 times that many, depending on regional differences.

In 1975, using the most conservative figures, Carole W. Offir estimated that "the chances of a Los Angeles woman meeting a rapist at some time during a 30-year period is about one in ten." By the 1990s this figure had been revised to one in three. Currently, the chances of a woman living in Los Angeles being sexually assaulted may be approaching 50%. And this figure does not include the nonsexual assaults such as battery, assault with deadly weapons, murder, attempted murder, etc.

The Male Rape Victim

Women are not the only rape targets. A growing number of male victims are assaulted by male rapists. Female rapists attacking male victims do occur but so infrequently that such incidents are tiny sociological problems compared with male-on-female and male-on-male rapes.

Male rape victims are typically in their teens and are raped by men in their 20s. The vast majority of suspects have spent time in jails where male-on-male rapes are daily occurrences.

The Los Angeles County Sheriff's Department, for instance, reports a case of two teenage boys—a 15 year-old and a 16 year-old—who were severely beaten and raped by two hitchhiking male suspects. The 16 year-old was driving his father's car when the boys decided to stop and give the two suspects a ride. The suspects hijacked the car, kidnapped the boys and took them to an isolated brush area. The victims were repeatedly raped and beaten. They were then left semiconscious in the brush. We strongly recommend against hitchhiking or picking up hitchhikers regardless of whether you are male or female.

Older males can also be rape victims. For example, the Los Angeles Police Department has numerous reports about attractive women picking up male victims in bars. They lure their victims to a room at a hotel or motel where the male suspect is waiting. Once inside, the woman holds a gun on the victim while her male accomplice rapes him anally and orally.

The Rapist And His Victim

How do rapists and their victims differ from their non-raping and non-victim counterparts? Rapists, regardless of how they appear in movies, are not necessarily insane. Dr. Amir writes that the personalities of rapists <u>don't</u> seem to be any more disturbed, with respect to their sexual preferences, than are the personalities of men who commit other crimes and who don't rape.

The rapists studied were, however, different from other men in their greater tendency to express violence or rage. Rapists, as a group, use force or fear to accomplish their crime.

Approximately 75%-80% of rapists have some familiarity with their victims, usually knowing at least their first names.

Dr. Selkin points out that rapists seek easily accessible places where they feel relatively safe to carry out the rape. Thus many rapes occur in run-down sections of cities/towns and in places occupied by women living alone. Victims picked up as hitchhikers are often assaulted in the rapist's car, van, or in some desolate area. Basements or first-floor apartments are easier for rapists to enter than are second-story dwellings or relatively secure residences.

Most rapists are not murderers. The Los Angeles Police Department reports that less than one percent of all murders involve so-called sex offenses. In the relatively rare instances when the rapist murders his victim, the killing is done where the rapist feels safe from interference.

That most rapists seek easy victims is borne out by the fact that when confronted by resisting victims, the assault was usually thwarted. According to the statistics cited by Dr. Selkin, less than 9% of resisting victims studied sustained injuries worse than a cut or a bruise.

Based on his data, Dr. Selkin advocates resisting a man's unwanted advances right at the beginning of his approach to the victim. Carole Offir agrees with this, stating that more and more rape counselors and self-defense experts are advising potential victims to resist physically. Such resistance apparently disrupts the rapist's fantasied sequence of planned events thereby depriving him of a victim who acts according to the submitting role he imagines her to play.

In their 1985 book Pauline Bart and Patricia O'Brien recommend relying on a variety of strategies such as fleeing, fighting, yelling, reasoning with the assailant, etc. They conclude that the more strategies you use, the more likely it is that you'll succeed in fending off the attacker.

Dr. Selkin also cites data comparing successfully resisting victims with non-resisting victims. These data indicate that the resisters see themselves as socially more competent and more self-accepting. This strongly suggests that building confidence is the first line of defense a potential victim can strive for in order to maximize the likelihood of successfully fighting off an attacker.

Friendly and helpful women are the most vulnerable according to Dr. Selkin. One-fourth of the victims studied by him were responding to requests for help. Requests for directions, for a glass of water or for the use of the victim's telephone, give the rapist opportunities to estimate whether he is about to confront a non-resisting victim or a fighter who might injure him.

Rape victims do not provoke the attack upon them.

Provocations (i.e., the victim engaging in behaviors which precipitate the rapist's attack on her) actually play a negligible role in our society's rape problem. The Federal Commission on Crimes of Violence reports that less than 5% of documented rapes involved any behavior on the victim's part that might—with some stretch of the imagination—be construed as provocative.

Most rapes are intra-ethnic. Dr. Amir reports that over 90% of rapes involved rapists and victims of the same ethnic make up. With respect to inter-ethnic rapes, his data show an insignificantly greater proportion of White men attacking Black women, for instance, over Black men raping White women.

Psychology

Comparisons between rapists and non-rapists by researchers or psychologists/psychiatrists have revealed very little useful knowledge.

Rapists come from virtually all walks of life and age ranges. However, the bulk of them are between 16 and 26 years of age and almost all of them are male.

Abel, and his coworkers, compared jailed, convicted rapists with men jailed for non-rape sex offenses (e.g., child molestation). The sex offenders were compared with respect to their sexual arousal (using a penile strain gauge) in response to audio-tape descriptions of both rape and mutually enjoyable intercourse scenes.

The nonrapists were aroused by scenes of mutually enjoyable intercourse but not by the rape scenes. The rapists, however, were aroused by both the rape and mutually enjoyable intercourse scenes.

There is evidence that aggression/hostility and rape are somehow connected. Since the late 1970s a number of researchers (e.g., Rada, 1978) using self-report inventories found that brutally violent rapists scored higher on expressed hostility than did less-violent rapists. Another consistent finding is that both the more violent and the less violent rapists had significantly higher hostility scores than did the control group of "normals."

In 1969 the analysis of the motives of rapists by Cohen and his colleagues yielded knowledge about types of rapists which is still valid today. The Cohen study distinguishes between the following four types of rapists:

1. <u>Displaced-Aggression Type</u>: *This rapist is driven by aggression. He has an uncontrollable impulse to rape, usually after some stressful event involving a wife, girlfriend or mother. There is little or no sexual excitement, and the rape is for the purpose of degrading or harming the victim.*

2. <u>Compensation Type</u>: *This type of rapist is sexually excited but feels sexually inadequate. He*

uses force to achieve his sexual goals.

3. Impulsive Type: *This is an opportunistic rapist who begins without sexual or aggressive intentions when a victim, through no fault of her own, happens to appear in the situation. The rapist takes advantage of the opportunity. Often the rape occurs during some other crime, such as burglary or robbery. Typically the perpetrator feels no guilt or remorse with respect to the rape.*

4. Sex-Aggression Diffusion Type: *Sexual fantasies are blended with aggressive feelings for the rapist. He may perceive a victim's struggles as seductive. This rapist is often brutal and some times murders his victim.*

Based on figures studied by LAPD's Crime Prevention Specialist Officer Esta L. Yonce, approximately 30-35% of rapists are of the displaced-aggression type. Perhaps 20-25% make up the compensation type. About 15-25% may be of the impulsive type, and possibly as much as 10% comprise the sex-aggression type.

Chapter 2

Name:_____

Question 3

Briefly describe the role of hostility/aggression in rape.

Chapter 2

Name:_____

Using the remainder of this page discuss types of rapists.

After The Rape

What To Do If You Are Raped

If you are the victim of rape, you should contact the Police/Sheriff as quickly as possible. LAPD's Officer Esta Yonce said that the quicker the police are contacted the better are the chances of catching the rapist.

A growing number of police departments have women officers who specialize in working with rape victims on a 24-hour, 7-day per week basis. This is in recognition of many (although not all) victims' greater degree of discomfort when talking about their ordeal with male officers. In Los Angeles, for example, if the first officers to arrive at your scene are male, they will ask you if you want to talk to a female officer. If you tell them that you want a female officer, she will be provided to you. A growing number of police departments (such as LAPD) give their officers special training to develop sensitivity to, and understanding of, the plight of the rape victim.

In addition to describing the details of the crime to a

police officer, the victim will also be asked to undergo a medical examination in order to gather scientific/medical evidence which helps to convict the rapist. Therefore, the victim should not douche, shower, clean up, straighten the furniture, etc., while waiting for the police. By doing these things she may be destroying evidence which is critical for the conviction of the rapist.

Unfortunately the rules of evidence and various Supreme/Superior Court rulings are such that it is difficult for prosecutors to win convictions against rapists. Law enforcement efficiently identifies viable suspects, but getting courts to convict accused rapists is very difficult without scientific and medical evidence. The conviction rates in most jurisdictions are consequently disappointingly low. Conviction is especially difficult if the victim, understandably or inadvertently, wipes away evidence through douching, showering, etc.

The stress of rape often causes victims to momentarily forget some of the details which may be useful for the police investigation. Follow-up interviews are therefore often made later in quiet surroundings where the victim feels more at ease. Under such calmer circumstances relevant items of information are sometimes recalled.

The victim may also be shown photographs of possible suspects, and often an artist will make drawings of the rapist according to the victim's descriptions of him. Comparisons of police artists' drawings and actual photographs of the suspects consistently show how accurate the drawings can be.

If the rapist is identified, the District Attorney's Office may prosecute, in which case the victim will be asked to appear in court as a witness. Many women feel uncomfortable about the prospect of going to court fearing mistreatment in the courtroom. In the past women had good reasons for harboring such fears. However, recent legal and attitudinal developments have improved the way rape victims are treated. Los Angeles County Sheriff's Department's Sgt. Virginia Hawkins said that in her 10 years of dealing with rape victims and going to court with them, she observed very few cases where the victim might be considered to be mistreated.

Sometimes the rape victim is uncomfortable about calling the police directly. If you are nervous about calling the police, call your local Rape Crisis Hot Line/ Rape Crisis Center (typically found under Rape in the white pages of your local telephone directory). Most of the time you will reach an answering service which will immediately put you in contact with a counselor. A representative of the Los Angeles Rape Crisis Hot Line suggested that the victim contact a trusted friend or relative to be by her side when talking with the police or when going to the hospital.

Many rapists threaten to return, thereby confusing

and frightening the victim even further. The Hot Line representative suggested, therefore, that the victim who has been raped at home arrange for a close friend or relative to come and stay with her until she feels safe again. She could also stay with someone until she's comfortable about returning to her home. In spite of their threats, rapists don't usually return to assault the victim a second time.

Ms. Gail Aberbanel, a social worker at Santa Monica Hospital, said that hospitals are showing more concern for the plight of victims and are providing more opportunities for counseling. Such counseling helps the rape victim to psychologically cope with her ordeal and to help her recover more quickly.

Clubs, women's groups, apartment complex residents, schools/colleges, etc., that want to help educate their members and/or their communities about the problem of rape, can draw upon the resources of their local police department, their local rape crisis center or rape programs such as Santa Monica Hospital's or Northridge Hospital Medical Center's. Often these agencies and groups are ready to send knowledgeable speakers who will discuss these problems.

The Los Angeles Police Department, for example, has several free programs available to the public, including Neighborhood Watch programs, one-evening, hands-on self-defense workshops and the **Lady Beware** program which is specifically geared to rape. Many police agencies across the country have similar programs available to groups in their communities.

Also many nonprofit, private organizations provide free, or low cost, assistance to victims. **Victims For Victims**, for example, is a growing organization founded by actress Theresa Saldana. Ms. Saldana was almost stabbed to death in 1982 and because of that experience she became the prime energy behind this group. **Victims For Victims** deals with all kinds of victims as well as rape victims by providing counseling, self-defense classes, peer support groups, etc.

Psychology

The victim's emotional reactions to rape are varied (Brownmiller, 1975). She may cry, scream or tremble. There may be inappropriate outward calmness. Or, there may be outbursts of laughter or tears.

Rape victims rarely commit suicide or go insane. However, it's not unusual for their social relationships (family, friends, coworkers) to deteriorate, often leading to divorce or the alienation of other family members.

In their 1974 publication Medea and Thompson delineated three phases of the typical rape victim's post-traumatic behavior. Their descriptions of post-traumatic difficulties also applies to victims of other violent crimes and have been verified by numerous other researchers since the 1970s. The three phases are as follows:

1. **First Phase:** *This includes the initial reaction of shock, fear and irritability, and typically lasts from several days to several weeks.*

2. **Second Phase:** *Here the victim returns to her usual routines. However, her feelings are merely suppressed and not resolved. There is repressed anger, anxiety, guilt, etc. Some victims never leave this phase.*

3. **Third Phase:** *Here the victim no longer denies her feelings. There often are signs of depression as she realizes the reality of her insecure world. She resolves her feelings constructively sometimes becoming active in self defense, crime-prevention activities or rape-crisis counseling. Regardless of the phase she is in, it's best for her friends and relatives to stay calm and to give her a lot of support. Don't lecture her, don't advise her, don't pressure her. If she does talk about her experience and feelings, be calm, quiet, supportive, non-judgemental and be a ready listener.*

Chapter 3

Name:_____

Describe, and elaborate upon, the victim's emotional reactions to rape.

Chapter 3

Name:_____

Briefly describe the rape victim's long-term, post-traumatic behaviors.

Prevention And Confrontation

Avoiding Rape/Muggings

Rape is the fastest growing violent crime in America. However, other violent crimes (e.g., battery, assaults with deadly weapons, muggings, etc.,) are also on the increase. Recent FBI data indicate that in the U.S. the total number of violent crimes is approaching 2,000,000 per year. This means that in general (allowing for regional variations, etc.) we have a one in 130 chance of being violently confronted each year.

This is a far greater risk than being afflicted by a fatal disease such as cancer. The odds of a woman getting breast cancer for example is only three out of a thousand.

Most rapes occur in residences; over one-third in the victim's own home. Attackers are not heroes governed by a sense of fair play. On the contrary, they prey on the weak, the intoxicated, the very young, the very old, the incapacitated, and on people they know. In other words attackers go after the most vulnerable victims in places where the attacker thinks s/he is safe from interference. Lone women at home, hitchhiking or walking, for instance, are very vulnerable to attack.

But regardless of the situation, there is considerable evidence that intended victims who fight back will survive with fewer physical and emotional scars than do victims who submit. The evidence is very strong, for instance, that once approached by a possible rapist, resisting women survive the confrontation with less damage than do non-resisting women. Of all the women in Dr. Selkin's study, for example, who fought back, less than 9% received anything more than a superficial cut or bruise. And as Dr. Bart found, the more strategies (such as conversation, yelling, running or striking out) women use, the more successful they are defending themselves.

In this chapter, however, we will concentrate on avoiding or preventing confrontations, and what to do when facing an attacker. One major point to remember is that regardless of any safety precautions which you may implement, there is never any guarantee of 100% security. Precautions and safety recommendations in this chapter, or from any other source, increase the degree of your security; they do not **guarantee** your safety. However, even small decreases in security risk can, and often do, make the difference between being a victim, a non-victim, or a strong survivor.

Begin by making a home security check. Closely examine every possible means of entry into your apartment or house. Do not underestimate the cunning or ingenuity of rapists or burglars to find ways of entering your house. In one Los Angeles burglary, for example, the burglars entered a high security home through a "doggie-door." Although the rest of the home was secured with state-of-the-art alarm systems, the family pet's door was left unlocked. Make sure that you have adequate locks on all the main doors leading into your home. Read Chapter X for more details about home security.

Never pick up hitchhikers or hitchhike yourself. This is the safest strategy for anyone, particularly for women alone. According to Sgt. Pitkin of the Los Angeles Sheriff's Department, the high number of rapes in the Malibu area, for instance, is due to the vulnerability of hitchhiking women. Furthermore, male rape victims have often made themselves available to rapists through hitchhiking. You are courting danger when picking up hitchhiking strangers or when hitchhiking. It is easy for a hitchhiker to use a weapon in order to force your compliance.

Confronting The Rapist

Regardless of the precautions taken, there is still a chance of being assaulted—whether you are male or female. If you are confronted by a rapist, or any attacker for that matter, there are several ways you can respond. These responses range from fighting to submitting.

Rape experts disagree on what response is best. Some experts caution the potential victim about trying to fight. Ms. Gail Aberbanel of Santa Monica Hospital tends to hesitate advising women to fight when confronted by a rapist, especially when the assailant is armed. Sgt. Virginia Hawkins of the L.A. County Sheriff's Department also tends to be conservative, especially when it involves female rape victims facing a muscularly stronger attacker. She suggests that the decision to fight should be left up to the individual woman.

Virtually all experts agree that the victim should look for an opportunity to run. As soon as such an opportunity arises the victim should break loose and run while yelling, "Fire! Fire!"

Based on his extensive data Dr. Selkin believes that women should fight when confronted. He cites data about resisting women and concludes that,

> "...a clear refusal to cooperate, no matter what form it takes, is by far the best way of resisting a would-be rapist."

In his data, 30% of the women confronted by rapists successfully resisted their attackers. Twenty-four per cent of them ran away. Eighteen per cent fought the attacker and 15% screamed. Rapists, according to Selkin and such other experts as Susan Murdock seek vulnerable victims. Screaming, fighting, and running reduces the intended victim's vulnerability, making her a less desirable target for the rapist.

Dr. Selkin and Ms. Murdock believe that it's important for the resisting victim to resist right at the start of the rapist's approach: before the attack gains its full momentum. The sooner she presents him with determined, strong resistance, the more likely she will be able to stop him.

Selkin and Murdock both advise against going along with the rapist for any period of time and then turning on him. Such behavior by the victim may anger or frighten the rapist into escalating his attack.

Your best initial action when attacked is to scream and run if possible. Run toward populated and well-lit areas screaming as loudly as you can. If, however, you are in an unpopulated area (e.g., a park) you might not want to scream. Suppose you break loose, run and hide. You don't want your screams to tip him off to where you're hiding.

Many authorities advise yelling "Fire!" because this tends to elicit greater response from bystanders than does "**Help!**" or "**Rape!**" In fact an informal study was done some years back using professional actors in the streets of New York, Chicago and San Francisco. The tough looking male actor pretended to attack the diminutive female actress in several different locations at different times within each of the cities. Whenever she yelled "Help!" NOBODY did anything to help her; witnesses didn't even call the police. Out of all the times when she yelled "Rape!," only one man came to help— **but not her**. He was a rapist coming to help the actor whom he thought to be a fellow rapist.

However, the actress got one hundred per cent bystander response when she yelled "Fire!" People called the fire department, the police department and each other. Many ran into the street to find the non-existing fire. Unfortunately the state of our urban society is such that cries for help don't necessarily get help. But people have a vested interest in protecting themselves, their loved ones and their belongings from a fire. Yelling "**Fire!**" will bring official help as well as immediate attention. Usually attention and the chance of being caught will stop an attacker.

There are many attention-getting noise-makers on the market. Whistles, for example, can be attached to key rings or even bracelets. Don't hang a whistle around your neck because the attacker might strangle you with it. There also are noise-makers which when pulled apart emit a continuous, loud noise. After triggering the noise you can throw it away to make it difficult for the assailant to grab and break it. Such noise-generating devices not only attract attention, they also tend to confuse the attacker.

Selkin and Murdock both advise that the victim's attitude should be of determined refusal to be intimidated. Dr. Selkin suggests that the safest strategy for potential victims, especially women, is to be polite but business-like, cool and detached. A strong sense of self-respect is a natural deterrent to attackers. Women should refuse aid from, and avoid offering help to strange men.

Whether a woman should try to talk a rapist out of attacking her is a controversial point. Some experts recommend saying nothing and others advise making karate-type yells. In their book, Her Wits About Her, Denise Caignon and Gail Groves include several examples of survivors who talked the attacker out of carrying out his threats. In their scholarly publication, Stopping Rape, Pauline Bart and Patricia O'Brien, however, hesitate advising women to use talking as their sole strategy. Their data strongly suggest immediate physical resistance as a better alternative.

To succeed in dissuading an attacker the victim/survivor must be skilled in evaluating the attacker and tailoring the conversation to his needs. Most of us just don't have such refined social skills under the extremely stressful conditions of attack. Alternating strategies until you find one that works is a good approach. Thus if an attacker doesn't respond to a verbal command such as "leave me alone," the defender can run, hit or yell. If you talk to an attacker, do NOT plead with him. Bart and O'Brien found that emotional responses such as pleading, begging, crying, etc., resulted in rape more frequently than any other type of resistance. Asking for mercy makes you appear weak and thus an easier victim.

With respect to rape Sgt. Hawkins (Sheriff) believes that resistance is a function of a woman's personality. If she's a passive, non-fighter type, resistance would be out of character for her and therefore perhaps less effective. An active, feisty personality may, on the other hand, be more successful at resistance.

Security-conscious people should take stock of their own character. Increasing your own self-confidence and assertiveness develops attitudes which help you succeed when you resist. The activities of various women's groups, college programs, assertiveness workshops, martial arts, as well as books, can help you develop assertiveness and self-confidence.

Psychology

The findings of Burgess and Holstrom show that the victim's primary reaction when confronted by an attacker is fear. Specifically, fear of being killed. The rape victim's fear often motivates her to submit to her attacker, hoping that he will spare her life.

However, as Brownmiller points out, submission is no insurance against physical harm. There are many examples (Boston Strangler, Speck, etc.,) where the victims were maimed/murdered after they complied with the attackers' directives.

At times submissiveness somehow encourages the attacker to escalate the viciousness of his attack. Dr. Bart found that the strategies of pleading and passiveness caused the attacker to <u>increase</u> rather than decrease his violence. Both of these orientations demonstrate vulnerability, a trait criminals look for. Some attackers' deliberate strategy is to estimate how far they can go with a particular victim partly by how submissive she is.

Many attackers, though not all, don't want to get hurt—physically or legally. They will therefore choose as their target vulnerable and submissive victims.

The effects of fear include the following:

1. <u>Reduced Coordination:</u> *The victim is more likely to fumble when reaching for a weapon or to stumble when attempting to run.*

2. <u>Reduction in Decision Quality:</u> *On the spot de-*

cisions (e.g., fight-and-run, talk-and-run, run only, submit, etc.,) are made more slowly, giving the attacker more time/advantage. The victim is also likely to make less than optimum decisions (e.g., attempting to run while trapped in a culde-sac and thereby giving away the intention to resist).

3. Narrowed Vision/Audition: *The victim often focuses on the threatening attacker. She may hear only him instead of the distant voices of possible rescuers. Or she may see only him and not possible escape routes.*

4. Muscle Tightening: *Tight muscles can interfere with any attempt to fight or run.*

Many experts, including Robert Barthol (ex-FBI agent and self-defense trainer with the California Highway Patrol), recommend "stress training." This includes vivid, mental rehearsals of fight/flight situations. During these mental rehearsals, relax the body muscles and defocus your vision (i.e., don't focus your sight at any one object). Stress training can also include regular practice of self-defense moves while visualizing being under attack or being threatened.

Chapter 4

Name:_____

Question 7

Discuss the impact of fear during an assault.

Chapter 4

Name:_____

Question 8

Briefly describe ways of controlling fear.

The Fighting Survivor - Armed

Introduction To Weapons

Weapons are instruments we can use for defensive or offensive combat. As defensive instruments we can consider weapons to be tools for survival. For the average person, weapons can range in degree of complexity from a simple stick to a semi-automatic gun.

When under attack there are many items around the house which the defender can use as hand-held weapons, such as sharp pencils, keys, bottles, etc. These weapons can be used as an extension of one's arm for striking, jabbing or stabbing the attacker. They can also be thrown at the attacker.

The successful use of any kind of weapon depends on four requisites: First of all you must be willing to use the weapon. Second, the weapon must be readily available to you. Thirdly, you should be skilled in the use of the weapon and fourth, we recommend having at least some skill in unarmed combat before you attempt to use a weapon. We will address these points in the next sections.

Weapons And Hesitancy To Use Them

Over 30 years of women's self-defense teaching at Los Angeles Southwest College, Los Angeles Pierce College and numerous LAPD self-defense workshops as well as teaching family oriented self-defense and karate classes at Learning Tree University, California Graduate Institute, at UCLA and at numerous other locations, have highlighted one crucial problem that many people face when confronted by an assailant. Whatever the causes (and apparently for more women than men) there is a hesitancy to hurt another—even if the other is an attacker.

A major survey study commissioned by the U.S. military found that only 35% of WWII, frontline troops admitted to aiming their weapons at enemy soldiers—even while under fire themselves.

Hesitancy to fight can give the attacker enough time to complete his assault. It also gives the attacker the opportunity to escalate the viciousness of his attack. Hesitancy, further, slows down the defender's counterattack.

Our many exposures to a wide variety of victims by way of our LAPD experiences and through our self-defense/karate classes at various other institutions show us the value of yelling to overcome the inhibitions against harming an attacker. In fact yelling during your defensive actions has several known advantages:

1. *It can attract attention.*

2. *By reducing the hesitancy to hurt, it allows the victim to counterattack with greater vigor.*

3. *Yelling can startle an attacker, giving the victim more time to counterattack and run.*

4. *If the yelling accompanies specific defensive moves (e.g., while jabbing fingers into the attacker's eyes), these moves will be stronger in the same way that grunting helps lift heavier objects.*

Once you decide to fight, yell loud, karate-type sounds as you strike into your assailant. Next, yell "Fire! Fire!" as you run toward a safe place.

Availability Of Weapons

Often a victim doesn't even know that he or she is under attack until the attack is in progress. In this case you don't have the time to reach for a weapon in order to use it. There are many women, for example, who carry mace, knitting needles, even loaded handguns, in their purse expecting to have the time to pull these weapons out while being attacked.

Some people decide to carry such illegal weapons as guns, clubs, daggers, etc. Such weapons can get the victim into legal difficulties. Perhaps some of our readers remember hearing about the San Francisco woman who used an illegal dagger to defend herself against an attacker. She was arrested for carrying the illegal weapon. Although the so-called subway "vigilante" in New York City was not prosecuted for shooting three of his four attackers, he was, however, convicted for illegally carrying a handgun.

There are a growing number of reports indicating that teargas doesn't always work. Many victims, for instance, were raped after they sprayed teargas directly into the attacker's eyes. On the other hand, some intended victims have successfully used teargas to repel attackers. We recommend pepper-spray over teargas because pepperspray is more likely to be effective.

Thus, the decision to rely on weapons, such as teargas or pepper-spray, has to be an individual one given the particular situation the victim is thrust into.

At home, a person who decides to fight when confronted by an attacker often has some kind of weapon within reach. Keys, bottle, cup of coffee, purse, etc., are all potential weapons. There are many items you can throw at your assailant such as a lamp, vase, book, or anything you can get a hold of.

Skill With Weapons

Whatever weapons you might think about using, you ideally should get some training and practice in their use. Even highly trained shooters, for example, under the stress of an attack can shoot so inaccurately that they accidentally shoot themselves or their loved ones without hitting the assailant. The same can be said of cutting weapons, such as knives, or blunt weapons, such as clubs or bats. In their excitement, would-be defenders have been known to cut or hit themselves by mistake.

Whatever the weapon of your choice you should practice regularly with it to reduce the risk of tragic accidents. This is especially true for lethal weapons such as guns.

Unarmed Combat Before Weapons

The biggest problem with weapons is that unless you have had enough training in some type of unarmed combat, the chances are quite good that the weapon can be taken away from you and used against you. If you decide to carry a deadly weapon—whether legally or illegally—you risk having it used against you by your assailant.

Keep in mind that nationwide the average police officer on the street is bigger, stronger, better trained and more street-wise than is the average civilian. Yet according to FBI statistics, each year about 10% to 20% of police officers who are shot on duty are shot with their own guns that have been taken away from them. And if you don't have time to produce your weapon while under attack you have nothing but your unarmed fighting skills to rely on.

Furthermore, the bulk of attacks occur in relatively confined and inconvenient locations where the victim is being crowded by the attacker. If you are constrained by the attacker, it is also more difficult to produce a weapon, and you are then forced, again, to rely on your weaponless fighting skills.

Weapons

Some people keep loaded guns inside their home. Before doing this yourself, consider that burglars/rapists may find the gun and use it against you. Or they may steal it and use it later. Furthermore your children, or visiting children, may find, play with and accidentally shoot someone with your gun. Each year about 8000 children are accidentally killed, and about 50 of these die because of gun-related accidents. Although this type of accident is relatively rare, it contradicts your defensive intent in having the gun. Furthermore, you could be held legally liable for criminal negligence. Firearms are dangerous, and you should keep this in mind when owning a gun of any kind.

Should you decide in favor of gun ownership, consult a reputable gun dealer, your local shooting range or your local police department for information about where to get the proper training for use of your weapon. You can also check with the local chapter of the National Rifle Association (NRA) for advice. For information about programs in your locality you can write or call them at, National Rifle Association of America 1600 Rhode Island Avenue N.W., Washington, D.C. 20036. Telephone: (202) 828 - 6000

Using a gun accurately and safely is not nearly as easy as the movies make it look. We therefore recommend that you regularly take time out for training, and updating, in the safe and defensive use of your gun. Some authorities, such as the late Sheriff Peter Pitches of Los Angeles, recommend that people should not rely on handguns to protect their homes. Rather, they recommend using shotguns because they require somewhat less training/practice than do handguns.

One final thought about gun ownership: although excellent weapons for the skilled and cautious user, guns are very dangerous and accidental maimings and killings do occur when they are improperly handled.

Esta L. Yonce, an LAPD crime prevention specialist, recommends a simple, "T"-type corkscrew as a legal weapon. It can be held with firmness and leverage while being used to cut, gouge and scrape. See photographs 5.1 and 5.2.

Whatever weapon(s), if any, you decide on, don't give the aggressor any warning by brandishing it prior to defending yourself with it. Counterattack immediately so that the attacker does not have time to second-guess your defense, or to intensify his attack.

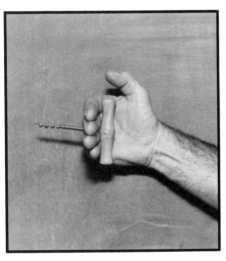

5.1. Gripping the "T" type corkscrew

Keys are very useful, weapons. Stick one or more keys between your fingers and jab, cut, or scrape until you can get away. When scraping your keys across the attacker's eyes, for example, move your fist so that the pressure on the keys is against the fingers and not in the direc-

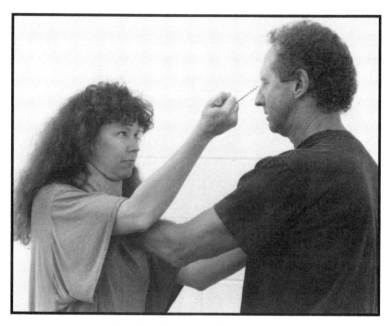

5.2. Gouging with the corkscrew

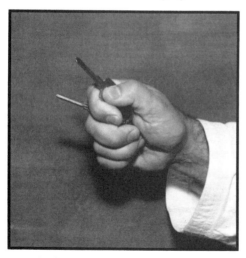

5.3. Grasping keys for self-defense

tion of the spaces between the fingers or they will slip and rotate until they are useless as weapons. See photographs 5.3 and 5.4.

When alone and approaching your house/apartment or your parked car, carry your keys so

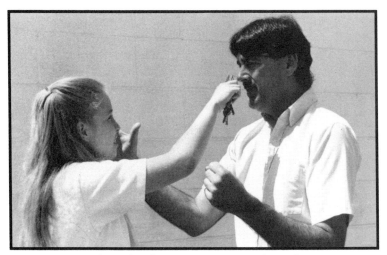

5.4. Scraping keys across an attacker's face

that they protrude from your knuckles through the spaces between your fingers. As you approach your parked car, for instance, your car key should be between your thumb and index finger for quick insertion into the car door's lock, or for quick counterattack if assaulted.

At home almost anything you can grab can be used as a weapon. You can throw or hit with bottles, vases, crockery, lamps, books, speakers, or anything which can make an impact upon, or distract an attacker. Again, yell as loud as you can throughout your counterattack. Many people own dogs for protection. A small barking dog is recommended for smaller apartments. Burglars and rapists don't like noisy, little dogs that can hide between, and under, furniture while continuing with attention-getting barking.

If you have sufficient room for a larger dog, just about any mutt from a well-kept pound will provide you with a good barking alarm which can deter an intruder. If you want to invest in a trained guard or attack dog, be prepared to spend at least $1000.00 and up. Make sure that you buy such animals from established and reputable trainers. Ill-trained dogs are dangerous to you and your family. Unscrupulous dealers will sometimes repeatedly beat a spirited dog until it becomes vicious, and then they'll try to pass these animals off to potential buyers as "trained" guard dogs. Such dogs can be very dangerous or useless.

Even well-trained guard/attack dogs should be kept in places enclosed by walls or fencing to minimize the risk of innocent people being hurt. The dog owner can be criminally and/or civilly liable for injuries caused by the dog.

Psychology

The question as to whether men and women are consistently different from each other with respect to abilities and personality traits, including aggressiveness, has been discussed for ages. However, systematic and relatively sophisticated studies of gender differences are rather recent. In the 1970s, Maccoby and Jacklin did a monumental review of over 2000 books and research articles and found very few consistent differences between men and women.

Aggression seems to be one area of difference between sexes. Boys display more verbal and physical aggression than do girls from about the age of two onwards. This gender difference was also observed within almost every culture and subculture that was studied. Some psychologists (Feschbach and Feschbach, 1973) believe that gender differences in aggression are due to social learning. Other behavioral scientists (Maccoby and Jacklin, 1974; Titley and Viney, 1969; Fox, 1983) believe that females are less aggressive than males because of biological differences.

Biochemical studies indicate that young female mice and humans develop more "male-type" aggressive behaviors when injected with testosterone (a male sex hormone). Any question regarding whether testosterone levels determine aggressive behaviors or whether aggressive behaviors influence testosterone concentrations is still unanswered.

However, regardless of the causes/antecedents of differences in aggressiveness between men and women, most psychologists believe that we can be trained to modify aggression. Most self-defense experts believe that women as well as men can, with sufficient training, repel serious attacks, and there are an overwhelming number of documented cases supporting this belief. The "Stress Training" referred to in Chapter IV is an example of training to respond more appropriately to danger for both men and women.

Chapter 5

Name:_____

Question 9

Describe gender differences, if any, in aggression.

Chapter 5

Name:_____

Question 10

Is aggression inborn or learned? Discuss and describe.

CHAPTER 6

The Fighting Survivor - Unarmed

Whenever possible, you want to prevent yourself from being attacked and to avoid situations and people who may become vicious. If you can escape from a confrontation, running and yelling "Fire!, Fire!" at the top of your lungs is a good defense. However, sometimes you are cornered. If there are no weapons within reach, you must make an important decision: To fight, unarmed, or to submit.

As noted in Chapter IV, with the ever-present caveats, a growing number of authorities are advocating fighting in most attack situations. R. Warshaw in a *Woman's Day* article, for example, describes the experiences of five women who survived because they fought back.

Another self-defense expert, Ms. Murdock, is quoted by BLACK BELT Magazine (January, 1977, page 95):

"To deny women this knowledge (i.e., self-defense) and to advocate their submission is to support their continuing victimization."

Furthermore, those who advise women to fight agree that the counterattack should occur right at the start of the attacker's approach.

To defend yourself, focus on your strengths and your attacker's weaknesses. For example, sharp fingernails and high heels can be used to your advantage. If you are small, speed and dexterity are strengths you can capitalize on. Intent is also in your favor. A good concept to remember that will augment your strength and fighting spirit is:

My will to survive is greater than
his (or anyone's) desire to harm me.

In most situations, you will be able to reach several vulnerable parts of your attacker's body. Where should you aim first? Choose openings that are available and sensitive.

Your attacker's face, for example, will generally be unprotected because he needs to see you to attack. Blows into the eyes, nose, mouth and throat can be effective especially if you strike hard and fast. On the side, the ears, temple and jaw are vulnerable.

The face is a good first choice for self defense because it has so many vulnerable parts. Another sensitive area is the groin, especially since you can reach it with both your legs (feet and knees) and your arms (fingers and hands). However, the groin is rather well protected by the thighs, and some men can take a hard kick to the crotch without being incapacitated. Therefore if you deliver a blow to the groin, be prepared to follow up with a second move to another vulnerable area, for example a jab into the assailant's eyes or a strike into the nose or throat.

Your assailant's knees are also relatively fragile, particularly from the side. A blow to the knee can knock your attacker down, giving you time to run while screaming "Fire! Fire!"

Other parts of your attacker's body, such as the stomach, shoulders and legs are less vulnerable. By striking into these areas, your defense may be ineffective and may incite your assailant to escalate his attack. Don't waste time. Always choose the most sensitive part of your attacker's body that you can reach.

On the other hand, with careful aim and with strong intent, your blows into any part of an assailant's body can disrupt his plan, giving you time to break loose, strike his face and run. Less vulnerable areas to aim for include the instep of the foot (especially if you are wearing sharp or hard heels), the lower ribs, the kidneys (just under the lower ribs on a person's back), the arm pit and the collar bone.

Remember, if one defense strategy doesn't work, keep trying with different moves until you find one that does the job. That brings up another question. What parts of your body can you use for self defense?

Almost every part of the human body has been used in self defense from head butts to kicking, scratching, biting, hip shoves and elbow strikes. But for the best results, again, plan to use your most effective physical tools against your attacker's most vulnerable areas. Fingers, hands, knees and feet are the best tools to start with because they each have several winning attributes:

1. *These are parts of your body that you are most familiar with, and*

2. *Being at the extremities, these body parts combine strength and speed.*

It's a very natural reaction to use your hands to help you break loose from an attacker. Avoid struggling with your assailant where you are pitting your strength against his. Keep in mind that he thinks he can take you. If he doubted his power over you, he would choose another victim. Instead of wrestling or grappling with an attacker who has grabbed you, go with his weight and strike into

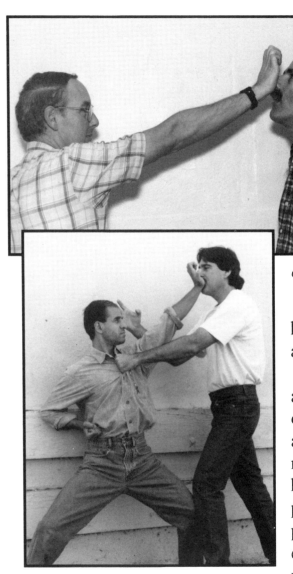

6.1. Palm-heel
strike to the
nose.

6.2. Nose-level, palm-heel strike sideward.

his body hard and fast.

For example, you can hit the assailant's nose with the heel of your palm. This is particularly effective if you step toward your opponent so that your body weight is behind your hand

The Fighting Survivor - Unarmed   *63*

6.3. Finger-jab
to the eyes.

and arm. Being at the end of your arm, the heel of your palm is often stronger than a regular punch. Also, using this technique you are less likely to injure your

6.4. Use of finger-jab against a frontal attack.

knuckles which are relatively fragile. See photographs

6.1 and 6.2. Even a very powerful man usually does not have a neck strong enough to withstand a hard palm-

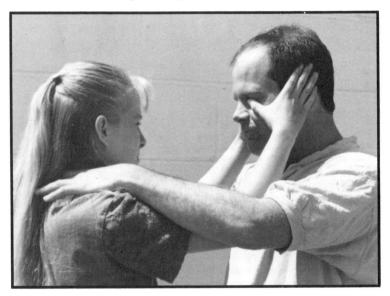

6.5. Eye-gouge using thumbs.

heel strike to the chin or nose.

You can also jab your fingers into your assailant's face and eyes with speed and power. When jabbing with your fingers, they should be somewhat spread apart (see photographs 6.3 and 6.4) and you should use <u>all</u> the fingers not just two. This way the chances are very good that at least one of the fingers will reach its mark. Jab as fast and hard as you can.

The objective is to stop an attack which could lead to your brutalization. If you break a finger or blind the

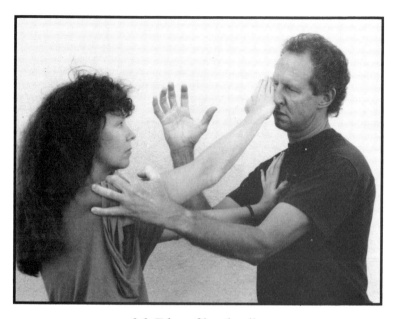

6.6. Edge of hand strike.

attacker while you are defending yourself that is a consequence the attacker has imposed on you. You have
the right to defend yourself, and the assailant is a threat
to your life and limb.

The thumb eye-gouge is another effective method
against a frontal attack. As shown in photograph 6.5,
you use your hands to stabilize the attacker's head as
you shove your thumbs into his eyes as hard and fast as
you can. Don't just think in terms of jamming at his
eyes, but instead, vividly visualize "DRIVING
THROUGH THE EYES AND THROUGH THE
BACK OF HIS SKULL." This mental imagery of driv-

6.7. Knee strike application.

ing through his head will give you much more power.

Striking with the edge of your hand (the old "judo chop") can also be effective when delivered crosswise into the attacker's temple or throat (see photograph 6.6). It can also be damaging when brought downward into the assailant's collarbone or to the inside of his arm at the elbow.

Your knee can also be a formidable weapon especially against aggressors who are in the process of trying to grab you. To execute a proper knee-strike you bring your heel up toward your buttocks as you ram your knee into the assailant's groin (see photograph 6.7).

Stomping, or kicking, hard into the assailant's knee is also an effective method of incapacitating him giving you time to run while screaming, "Fire! Fire!" (see pho-

6.8. *Stomping into the attacker's knee.*

tograph 6.8).

It is good to alternate hand and leg techniques to keep your opponent off guard. For example, if you hit a man in the nose with a palm-heel strike, follow up with a swift knee strike to the groin or a kick or stomp into the knee-joint. He may well be discouraged long enough for you to run.

If you want to become proficient in unarmed fighting, there is no substitute for steady practice in a martial art at a reputable studio. Unfortunately, however, most people don't undertake such training and have to rely on their "natural" defenses such as screaming, scratching, biting, etc.

If you don't plan to train in a martial art, you might seriously consider participating in short-term self-defense courses at your local community college, YMCA, police department or woman's group.

At the very minimum you should <u>think</u> about defending yourself. Pre-planning strategies is better than no planning. The work of Bart and O'Brien, for example, strongly suggests that the more strategies women have thought about or practiced prior to being attacked, the greater are their chances of survival with a minimum of physical and psychological trauma.

For rape situations, local women's groups or knowledgeable friends can help you appreciate self-defense at a level that is comfortable for you.

One caveat regarding "knowledgeable" friends. Often friends think they know about real world self defense when they really don't. So we suggest "chose your friends carefully."

Psychology

Learning to respond with the proper defensive moves requires regular and repetitive practice. Ideally you **overlearn** the moves by practicing them to mastery because then you don't need to take time to think about your defense—you just do it.

When first practicing the self-defense moves, you will need to exercise conscious effort. However, repeated and frequent practice will gradually allow you to perform them more and more smoothly with less and less conscious involvement. This, in turn, means that you will react more quickly and more effectively when facing a serious attacker.

The research of many psychologists (e.g., P. London) indicates that distributed practice is superior to massed practice. In other words, mastery of self-defense skills is more likely if the practice sessions are spaced out rather than bunched together. The chances are that practicing a few minutes a day, every other day, is all you will need for handling the typical attacks as reported to the police.

Chapter 6

Name:_____

Question 11

Discuss the importance of overlearning when practicing any skill.

Chapter 6

Name:_____

Question 12

Discuss the relative merits of massed versus distributed practice.

Learning To Fight

The Martial Artist

Martial arts training is highly recommended for self-defense for anyone, at any age and for any size. Martial arts training is also an excellent form of exercise. At the Topanga-Valley Karate School in Canoga Park, for instance, the karateka (students) in the adult classes are typically in their 30s, 40s and 50s—a couple of them are in their 70s. Many are highly educated professionals and about half are women.

Obviously, given your age and particular body, the better conditioned you are, and the more sophisticated your skills in the martial arts, the more successful you will be in warding off an attacker. If you are not fit enough to either run or fight, you are indeed a very vulnerable victim. A couple of hours of exercise per week can make the difference between your life and death.

Once you have committed yourself to a program of exercise, you might consider training in a martial art, or taking self-defense classes, at a nearby studio or college. In an Executive Fitness (1989) article R. Birrer, M.D., is quoted as stating that coordination, flexibility, power, speed and strength are all developed by the practice of the martial arts.

Dr. Paffenbarger, of Stanford University, reported the results of his long-term study on the health benefits of exercise. His results show that those who burn 2000 calories per week through exercise suffer significantly fewer heart problems than those who burn fewer than 2000 weekly calories.

After studying a number of different, popular forms of exercise, Dr. Paffenbarger arranged them into three categories on the basis of how efficiently they cause the practitioner to burn up 2000 calories per week when done three different times each week: Best; moderately good; poor. He concluded that karate is one of the best activities for meeting the 2000 calories-per-week goal. Running (7 m.p.h.) and cross-country skiing were also included in the best exercise group.

Many colleges and universities offer low-cost courses in various systems of self-defense. Most of the University of California and California State College campuses, for example, offer Karate, Tae Kwon Do, Kung Fu, and self-defense classes. Some of the private universities also offer good classes. Stanford University, for instance, offers outstanding self-defense classes designed by 10th degree black belt Master Duke Moore.

An excellent place for some initial exposure to the martial arts/self-defense is through university or community college extension programs. Most of them have non-credit classes open to the general public. UCLA, Pierce College, Los Angeles Southwest College, San Francisco City College, etc., all offer self-defense/karate classes on a one-evening per week basis for a small service charge. Members of the Armed Forces usually have martial arts clubs available to them at the various military bases. A good resource about martial arts in the armed forces are Tae Kwon Do instructors Mr. Jerome Reitenbach or Ms. Sydney Reeser of the Reitenbach Institute at 6000 Mission Street, Daly City, California, 94014.

Various police/sheriff's departments offer free crime prevention and self-defense workshops to civilian groups. The Los Angeles Police Department, for instance, offers a variety of free programs to the general public. There is the **Lady Beware** program involving anti-rape demonstrations. LAPD also has the very effective **Neighborhood Watch** programs. The data clearly show that active, on-going neighborhood watch programs effectively reduce all kinds of crimes, including violent crimes.

For the last 20 years LAPD has also been offering free, one- evening, hands-on self-defense workshops. Civilian groups such as employee organizations, apartment dwellers, church groups, schools, colleges, etc., have availed themselves of these workshops by calling The Community Relations Office of their particular Division/Area.

After deciding to take up a martial art, there are several other decision you must make. First of all, you have to decide which martial art (Aikido, Kendo, Karate, Tae Kwon Do, Ju Jitsu, etc.,) to take up. You must then decide which school or studio (dojo) to train in. If you live in a community with few dojo, your choices are restricted. However, if you live in a medium or large size city, you usually have a tremendous variety of dojo to choose from. Regardless of where you train, be prepared to practice very hard for many years to approach mastery of the art you take up.

Although it takes years to master a martial art, your chances of surviving a fight are increased commensurate with just about any level of skill. Even a beginning student can successfully defend him/herself when attacked. For example, a Topanga-Valley Karate School student who weighed only 105 pounds knocked out a 185 pound known rapist who was wanted by the police of three counties for both rape and murder. At the time of her successful defense, she had trained in karate for only 3 months. Before this she had never been in a fight, and her primary motive for taking karate was its excellent exercise value.

In general, the more you train, the better you'll be able to defend yourself. And this is true for just about anyone at any age. A 9 year old girl who was a member of the junior class successfully defended herself and a same-aged friend against a very serious kidnap attempt. She used a self-defense routine that is regularly practiced at the Topanga-Valley Karate School. One of this school's adults after many years of constant practice passed his black belt test at age 74. A year later he successfully fought off two muggers who were considerably younger than him.

The hard-working, dedicated, steady student can usually achieve the black belt level (mastery of basics) in about 4 to 6 years. Of course the older, the more uncoordinated, or the poorer the physical condition of the student to begin with, the longer it takes to achieve the black belt level of proficiency. Some individuals take 7 to 10 years, and up, to achieve the rank of shodan (first level of black belt). The first level of black belt is usually awarded to students who have mastered certain basic techniques and concepts. If you count on three well-spent hours per week of training, it will take a minimum of 600 hours to attain the rank of Shodan at ' good, technique-based school.

The reader should be warned that there are no short-cuts to the mastery of fighting skills. Don't be fooled into paying high prices for low-quality instruction, or into a false sense of security by unscrupulous studio operators. Shop around. Your safety is at least as important as a new car or house. It's amazing how many people are fooled into paying a lot of money for their one to two year black belts while deluding themselves into believing that they're brilliant fighters.

Together with other experts (see Sports Illustrated, 1975) we estimate that about 95% of studios in our cities are either phony or are so sports-oriented that they cover material which is relatively ineffective in the street. Many sports-based tournaments occur every weekend where points are awarded for "tagging" (weak moves) rather than for authoritative techniques which could stop a real attacker. And these tournaments produce "champions" who have difficulty defending themselves during a real attack.

For self-defense purposes we therefore recommend looking for studios which emphasize self-defense over sport. Visit the school and see what kind of students it attracts. If it attracts mostly children and adolescents, it's likely to be phony. Stay away from contracts and be wary of chain schools. Also be wary of schools which produce "90-day wonders" (i.e., grind out so-called black belts within just a couple of years) because their standards may be too low. Low standards could mean sloppy, ineffective self-defense.

The issue of phony instructors is an important one because they could be teaching material which doesn't work in life-and-death situations. Whatever credentials they claim to have or show may not be authentic or verifiable. The **Valley** edition of the May 1, 1988, **Los Angeles Times**, for instance, contained an investigative article about a well-known martial arts instructor who made a number of claims about himself. According to the reporter none of the claims are verifiable. Maybe he is telling the truth about himself, but a staff reporter could find no proof.

You as consumer could have equal difficulty verifying an instructor's claims. Look for hard evidence such as photographs, videotapes, movies, etc., but most of all look at and talk to the adult students the studio attracts. If they tend to be well-informed, intelligent, successful adults you are likely to have walked into an authentic dojo.

Psychology

Mental practice is an important adjunct to the physical practice of the self-defense moves which you learn in a martial arts class. Many psychological studies and sport psychologists (Cratty; Lawther) indicate that complex psychomotor skills, such as self-defense skills, are enhanced through mental practice. Sometimes mental practice consists of imagining yourself performing the defensive moves. At other times your mental practice involves verbalizing the submovements of each defensive motion (e.g., finger-jab into the attacker's eyes). Your mental practice could also consist of imagining another person performing the defensive moves while you are standing back and observing.

Research indicates that mental practice:

1. *Produces faster learning than mere observation.*

2. *Is more useful when first learning the task.*

3. *Should not be done for very long. Not much longer than 5 minutes at a time.*

4. *When used in combination with physical practice, mental practice produces better results than does physical practice alone.*

5. *Is most effective with complex defensive moves when, for instance, putting together a combination of moves.*

When practicing the self-defense moves, then, you

Learning To Fight

should mentally visualize, as realistically as you can, an attacker. In addition to your physical practice, it is also advisable to do this mental practice at least once per week.

Chapter 7

Name:_____

Question 13

Describe the different ways mental practice is done.

Chapter 7

Name:_____

Briefly explain why a self-defense student might want
to engage in mental practice.

Starting Martial Arts Training*

Choosing A Martial Arts

Most metropolitan areas offer a variety of different martial arts to interested students. This particular section of this chapter reviews some of the more commonly found martial arts, and the next section of this chapter deals with the problem of choosing a particular studio (or dojo).

A common question is, "What's the difference between judo and karate?" The partial answer is that judo is a grappling, throwing and holding art, whereas karate is a kick-and-punch art.* Thus, to the beginner, the

*Since this chapter is written for the beginner, much of its content is oversimplified. The sophisticate in the martial arts is asked to keep this in mind when reading this chapter. The descriptions of various arts herein are written for the beginners' eyes.

difference between karate and judo resembles the difference between boxing (karate) and wrestling (judo).

Note that in karate the person punching or kicking avoids actually hitting or kicking his/her partner by stopping the move just short of contact. The so-called full-contact "karate" seen by some on television or in movies is not karate at all. The resemblance to karate is strictly superficial. The "full-contact" sports are more like kick-boxing.

8.1. Proper body alignment between target and floor.

8.2. Insufficient body support for the punch.

Karate, especially traditional approaches to it, is unique in the sense that it emphasizes technique factors which underly such moves as strikes, blocks, kicks, etc. These technique factors give the karate practitioner speed, power, and impact regardless of his/her size. Examples of techniques (vs. moves) include body alignment and hip/body rotation. Photograph 8.1 shows, for instance, the proper alignment of the body between the target and the floor. Photograph 8.2 shows the wrong way of ending a punch because there is insufficient support from the body. And photograph 8.3 shows the right way of ending a punch because of the body support.

Alignment and hip/body rotation to back up fighting moves are only two of many technique factors knowledgeable karate instructors emphasize. These technique factors allow a small person to defend him/herself against a larger attacker without relying on unusual muscular strength or youthful reaction times. This makes it possible for older, slower, smaller, at times disabled karateka to successfully defend themselves against muscularly powerful attackers.

However, these technique factors take a lot of practice and mental concentration to master, and many people are just unwilling to discipline themselves to focus on the details of these techniques. This is unfortunate because they will therefore opt to do nothing of self-defense value or attend ersatz studios that emphasize muscular strength and moves rather than techniques. For further information about traditional karate/self-defense the reader is referred to Weiss, B., and Weiss, H. **SELF-DEFENSE FOR EVERYBODY: A primer in applied karate**. (Hiles & Hardin, 1992).

Some students prefer the sense of rapid progress they gain from training at a studio which emphasizes muscular strength and moves rather than techniques. While

8.3. Proper body support for the punch.

movement training may be less effective for street defense, it is still valuable for mind/body coordination, awareness, and physical health.

Team sports (basketball, volleyball, baseball, soccer, etc.) and partner sports (tennis, raquetball, etc.) also develop mind/body coordination and physical endurance. In addition, these activities, like martial arts, teach you to judge and respond to body movement around you. Even in individual sports (bicycling, aerobics, swimming, golf, mountain climbing, skiing, etc.) the mind and body must judge the environment and evaluate choices in order to avoid injury and to have the best experience. Any kind of regular practice to improve physical skill and movement awareness increases your self-defense capacity.

The various martial arts might be described in terms of the mix of grappling (i.e., grabbing and wrestling) and kick-and-punch (hitting/striking) they emphasize for the beginning student. Western examples would include wrestling (College or Olympic) on the grappling end and boxing on the hitting/striking end.

The Asian martial arts, however, are more suited for the average person and we will focus on these. What follows is a partial list—in alphabetical order—of some of the better known martial arts with a brief description of each.

Aikido/Aiki-Jutsu

Aikido and Aiki-jutsu (spelling of Jutsu will vary) are on the grappling side of the martial arts. There are many wrist movements to evade or turn attacks. Aikido also emphasizes a way of mental concentration or flow, called Ki, that increases the efficacy of the techniques.

Hapkido

This art includes elements of both throwing and kick-and-punch. The training usually emphasizes throwing and holding techniques together with high and varied kicks.

Judo

*Judo is primarily a grappling **sport** and, the way it is typically taught, has little immediate self-defense applicability. The rules allow the contestants to try to sweep, throw or pin one another to score points. With its repeated pounding into the mat, it is a very rough sport. Tenth degree black belt master Mr. Duke Moore, therefore, recommends starting it only if you are relatively young (under 25 years old). See photographs 8.4 and 8.5*

Ju-Jutsu

Ju-Jutsu (aka Ju-Jitsu, Jiu-Jutsu, Ju-Jiutsu, etc.), which is often confused with judo, basically consists of all the judo moves plus wrist and joint twists/locks, pressure points and, at times, some kick-and-punch moves. Many Ju-Jutsu moves have sound self-defense applicability which may explain its recent resurgence of popularity. See photograph 8.6.

Karate

There are many different styles of karate (e.g., Shotokan, Shori-ryu, Shorei-ryu, Goju-ryu, Shorin-ryu, Wado-ryu, Shito-ryu, etc.), all of which emphasize

8.4 & 8.5. Using judo/ju-jutsu techniques, 10th degree blackbelt master Dr. Duke Moore, escapes from a stranglehold applied by 8th degree blackbelt Dr. Bernd Weiss.

kick-and-punch type moves, although most include at least some grappling moves.

8.6. A ju-jitsu wrist twist technique as demonstrated by
7th degree black belt Dr. James Moses of Stanford University
as 6th degree black belt Dr. Abbas Daneshvari looks on.

The unique feature of most karate classes (although
not necessarily all) is the emphasis on technique factors to support the moves. A growing number of self-
defense experts recommend karate as the best, overall self-defense activity for the average person of any
age. A leading martial arts/self-defense expert of the
Los Angeles Police Department has field tested a variety of martial arts and strongly urges the study of
karate by police officers.

Kendo/Iaido

These are the arts of the Japanese sword. Iaido essentially involves well-choreographed moves with a real blade. Kendo is "fencing" using sticks instead of real swords. The practioners wear elaborate armor to protect themselves against the blows of the surrogate swords. Kendo has excellent self-defense application when the victim has access to a stick (or anything like a stick, e.g., broom).

Kung-Fu

Kung-Fu, Gung-Fu, Chuan-Fa, Wu-Shu, Chinese Boxing, etc., contains elements of kick-and-punch as well as grappling moves. There are hundreds of different systems or styles which tend to emphasize circular evasions and deflections. The student interested in Kung-Fu is advised to shop around to see which best fits his/her personality.

Because Kung-Fu has experienced much media coverage there are many charlatans claiming to teach some form of it. We therefore recommend extreme caution while shopping around. For information about Kung-Fu schools in your area you might call the editorial offices of Inside Kung Fu Magazine, Inside

Karate Magazine *or* Black Belt Magazine.

Ninjutsu

Ninjutsu came from feudal Japan's secret assassins who used a variety of moves and tools for stealth and attacking. The published descriptions of ninjutsu (as well as what we have seen) as practiced in the U.S. today indicate that the fighting moves of this art are a watered down version of ju-jutsu.

During our visits to Japan in the 1980s we were told by Okinawan and Japanese martial arts experts that the last known ninjutsu master died in 1950. In fact, they expressed amusement at the so-called American ninjutsu masters who claim to know the moves of this art since they would have been too young to have trained in it throughout the 1940s. Even if they were old enough to have been in post-war Japan they could not have trained long enough to acquire master status.

This seemes to be supported by the research of knowledgeable scholars such as H. Reid & M. Croucher (1983, p. 130) and D. Draeger (1980, p. 131). In fact, Donn Draeger, who is considered to be a top martial arts scholar, in his book Comprehensive Asian Fighting Arts makes the flat statement, "No ninja exist today." The first edition of this book is dated 1969.

Tae Kwon Do

Most (but not all) Tae Kwon Do instructors concentrate on the movement of kicks which makes it a useful activity for those relatively few self-defense situations in which the attacker is outside of your arms' reach. However, most self-defense situations (as reported to police departments) occur in confined spaces where the attacker is too close for full-range kicking to be effective. We therefore recommend that if you want to train in Tae Kwon Do for self-defense purposes, pick a studio which consistently adds karate-type arm techniques. The late John Pereira, for example, incorporated in his Wado Ki Kai system Karate for self-defense and Tae Kwon Do for those who enjoy these kicks.

Tang Soo Do

Tang Soo Do resembles karate in that the moves of these two arts are similar. However, most Tang Soo Do instructors (although not all of them) teach moves only and not technique factors. Adding to the beginning student's confusion is the fact that Tang Soo Do practitioners took their kata (choreographed forms consisting of defensive moves against imaginary multiple opponents) from various karate styles (especially Shotokan). But very few Tang Soo Do masters teach (although some talk about) the technique factors of karate.

T'ai Chi Chuan

As normally practiced, self-defense applications are usually not emphasized in T'ai Chi Chuan. The moves are fighting motions but are usually practiced in a dance-like way. This art is good exercise but is usually taught with little immediate self-defense applicability. There are, however, some instructors who teach full-speed, "combat" T'ai Chi which might have greater usefulness for self-defense. Los Angeles' Reverend Mitram Ware, for example, teaches Tai Chi for self-defense.

Hopefully this brief glance at some of the martial arts will provide the reader with an introduction to what is available. Once you decide to take up a martial art, you need to decide which art to take, and then you must choose the particular school to train in.

With respect to self-defense for women, or men attacked by a larger aggressor, it is advisable to select a kick-and-punch art which includes methods for close-in fighting. The grappling arts are somewhat more difficult to apply against a muscularly stronger aggressor. Many experts recommend karate because well-taught and well-practiced karate techniques allow the student to maximize impact with a minimum of muscular strength. Medea and Thompson write for example,

"We recommend karate rather than other Oriental military arts...Your endurance and general well-being will improve, your reflexes will sharpen, and you will develop automatic reactions."

8.7. T'ai Chi Chuan develops balance and body coordination as presented by Rev. Mitram Ware.

Choosing A Karate Studio

Finding a good karate school (or dojo in Japanese) is easier said than done. There are many charlatans teaching poor techniques that can actually be dangerous. Often their students are "psyched" into believing they are invincible.

Back in the 1970s Sports Illustrated, for example, published an authoritative article which contained the opinion that the vast majority of karate schools are phony. Today fakery in the martial arts is quite rampant (See L.A. Times' Valley section, 1988,

May 1: 4-11; also see the editorial comments and letters to the editor in recent issues of **Black Belt Magazine**).

Before deciding on a school, make sure you shop around and spend at least several hours at each school observing the training. Talk to the students to find out about their school and instructor(s). Be wary if the students are in excessive awe of their teacher as though s/he is an invincible guru. Try to evaluate, as best as you can, how effective the moves that are being taught actually are (or would be) against a bigger or stronger adversary.

There is no substitute for dedicated, steady, practice of good techniques under competent instruction for the development of sound fighting skills. Don't let the fakers persuade you to believe that you can learn the deadly "secrets" of their fighting system over night. There are no secrets other than techniques which make the desired impact upon the aggressor. There are no shortcuts to the mastery of karate or any martial art. Many so-called experts will tell you that they earned their black belts with a year of everyday training. The chances are that they are fooling you or, worse still, themselves. It takes the body—its musculature and its nervous system—**time** to learn the complicated skills inherent in the martial arts. Therefore there is a ceiling to how much you can accelerate your skill development by everyday training.

It is apalling how many otherwise intelligent people are willing to buy a 1-year, $2,500.00, black belt guaranteed course from unscrupulous, so-called "masters."

Again, don't confuse sports-oriented martial arts training with self-defense. Many point-scoring tournament moves are useless against muscularly stronger street fighters. There are many acrobatic, flashy moves being taught which look impressive but are really very weak. The beginning student will have to use good judgement while shopping around and observing schools. Stay away from schools which don't give spectators the opportunity to observe classes.

There is no necessary relationship between the quality of instruction and the cost of lessons. Some dojo charge very little for outstanding instruction. Others charge very high fees for poor teaching. Look for a sensei (i.e., teacher) who is more interested in spreading/imparting the art than in parting your money from you. By the time you pay all the obvious and hidden costs many studios in the Los Angeles area end up charging you well over $100.00 per month. Dojo charging less than $60.00 per month are rare and could be quite good.

Many dojo offer contracts. Be careful of these. Unfortunately, many dojo are begun by fast money fly-by-nighters. Even most well-intentioned martial arts instructors typically don't last much longer than a couple of years. Well-established schools which have been in existence for 10 years or more with, therefore, a skilled core of black & brown belts are few and far between and rarely sell contracts.

Also beware of complete courses such as buying a brown/red belt or black belt program. For example a family of four (father, mother, teenaged daughter and son) for a large sum of money bought a brown belt course for the whole family. Nine months later they were "tested," passed to brown belt, and told that the contract had been met. Because the studio belonged to a major chain run by a famous name and because they compared themselves to others at the same level, the family believed themselves to possess brown belt skills. However, when they were guests at a legitimate studio (where it takes even talented people 2-3 years to make brown belt) they saw how much more effective these other students were and realized they had been cheated. They were lucky to discover their weaknesses so easily rather than by having to fight for their lives in the street. Caveat emptor.

The student is strongly advised to avoid sadistic instructors who foster a belligerent atmosphere in the studio. Such an atmosphere is, unfortunately, all too common and is reflected in high injury rates and low skill levels. Under sensible instruction, training hours lost due to injuries are extremely low while the students' skills are high for each rank.

Even after you achieve considerable proficiency in a martial art, you should never underestimate your assailant. Avoid a confrontation whenever possible. Run if you can. Fight only if you have absolutely no other choice.

Psychology

Consumer psychology gives us some clues regarding the success—usually short-lived but at times profitable—enjoyed by some martial arts charlatans (McCormick and Tiffin).

Our **perceptions** are influenced by our needs, and con artists provide us with what may appear to be **incentives** which are supposed to fulfill those needs.

Perception is the organization and interpretation of what we hear and see (Lawther). Needs are the internal, felt wants of individuals. Incentives are those things which are perceived by an individual as satisfying his needs.

According to Abraham Maslow among our most basic needs are physiological and safety needs. We want to feel safe, secure and invincible. Most of us go to great lengths to maintain the illusion of invincibility including the willingness to listen to the empty promises of the con artist.

If we perceive martial arts training as making us safe and secure, we may perceive the charlatan's impossible promises as being plausible. At this point he may easily separate us from our money.

The charlatan may have impressive looking credentials or associations which he may use to delude his customers into believing that they can actually learn faster than is humanly possible.

The victim's fantasies may read, "Wow! Sensei X (teacher) is affiliated with the great grandmaster Y, so it must be true that for a mere $3000.00 he can make me black belt in only 2 years, or can make my child a black belt by the time s/he is 9 years old."

Chapter 8

Name:_____

Question 15

Briefly describe the relationship between perception, needs and incentives.

Chapter 8

Name:_____

Question 16
Discuss how a charlatan might manipulate a victim.

Safety Away From Home

Safety On Foot

Avoid walking alone on the street especially at dusk or after dark. If you absolutely have to do this, there are a number of security precautions you can take.

Choose well-lighted and populated areas. Avoid such desolate areas as deserted alleyways, empty lots, vacant doorways, woods/shrubbery, stairways, and so on.

When carrying purses, pouches or wallets make sure they are of a design allowing you to grip them tightly. Shoulderbags should be carried with the flaps closed inward against the body. One hand could be placed on the flap to reduce a pickpocket's access to its contents.

If a man attacks you for your purse or wallet, you may just want to give it to him. The contents of a purse or wallet are not worth risking your life. If you decide to give up your purse, let go of it immediately, otherwise the robber/pursesnatcher may hurt you in the struggle.

Never leave your belongings unattended in public places such as markets, theaters or stores. Don't, for example, place your purse on the counter or in the shopping cart. Thieves look for such "abandoned" items and snatch them while you are momentarily distracted. Sometimes, in fact, they work in pairs. While one engages your attention, the other takes your property.

When inside a restroom cubicle don't place bags, purses, wallets, etc., on the floor or on the hook inside the door. A thief can easily reach under or over the door to remove whatever you have there. And these thieves can do this so quickly that by the time you react, they're already gone.

If your purse, wallet, jacket is stolen in a market, restroom or theater, immediately report it to the management and the police. Further, immediately change all the locks in your home, inform the credit card companies and change your checking account.

Sometimes thieves will burglarize your home after obtaining the keys and address from the stolen purse. To get you out of your home long enough to commit the burglary, they may call you and pretend to be employees of the establishment where your purse or wallet was stolen. Typically they will ask you to return in order to claim the missing property. Double check such a call by immediately telephoning the manager of the store or theater before you leave the house.

If you are a woman walking alone and men make rude and suggestive remarks to you, maintain a rejecting, confident and determined attitude. Such an attitude is likely to discourage them. This attitudinal show of strength has actually been field tested by a series of studies done by Dr. Frank Puskas, an international crime prevention specialist in private practice and co-author of the book **Psychology and Methods of Survival.** Don't maintain direct eye contact with them because they may misinterpret such contact as a challenge or "come on." We therefore recommend looking at their throat level while defocussing your vision. Our research indicates that this can be unsettling for a possible attacker or molester. Furthermore, visual defocussing allows you to be more cognizant of items in your whole visual field while at the same time setting your brain up for a quicker flight/fight response should you need it.

If the harassment gets out of hand, rapidly walk toward a well-lighted or populated area like a store or business and call the police. Note descriptions (approximate height, weight, coloring, etc.) of the men as well as any license plate numbers. Sometimes the men belong to a vehicle or site which has the business name/ phone number of their employer painted on it. Note the number and complain to the employer about the harassment. Most business owners are sensitive about their public image because their business depends on their reputation. And most of the time, phone complaints result in the cessation of harassment.

If a man is following you in his car while you are on foot, or if he is persistently trying to persuade you to get into his car, memorize his license number and walk away from the car in the opposite direction.

Rather than walking alone after dark, call a taxicab to either take you home or to wherever your car is parked. Don't wait at desolate bus stops at dusk or after dark. It's better to pay the cab fare than to risk life and limb.

Use judgment when going to the beach or to the movies alone. If you are alone, you can reduce risks by carefully choosing where you sit or swim. Immediately report any pest to the lifeguard, manager or usher.

Don't sunbathe or swim in desolate parts of the beach. Stay near family groups or near the lifeguard. In a theater sit in an aisle seat, preferably at the center aisle, whenever possible. If anyone abuses you verbally or tries to touch you improperly, complain to the management and take another seat.

If someone follows you on foot trying to persuade you to go with him, or is annoying you in any way, turn to face him and in a loud, clear voice shout at him to leave you alone. Yell if you have to. No response or a fear-response, may signal a rapist that he is confronting a vulnerable victim.

If whoever is harassing you starts to shove, push, or grab you, threatens you verbally or brandishes a weapon, you will need to use your judgment. At this point you might decide to yell, fight (e.g., thrusting your fingers into his eyes) and run. Run toward well-lighted, populated areas if available. If you can't find a populated spot while being pursued you might run to parked vehicles and climb under one, face upward (i.e., your back on the floor) and grab whatever parts of the underside of the car you can get a hold of. Usually you can also hook your feet into, or through, exposed parts of the chassis. While you hang on to the various parts of the vehicle, repeatedly scream "Fire! Fire! Fire!..." It is almost impossible for even a superstrong attacker to get down on all fours and from that position to pull you out from under the car or van. Vans are particularly good for this. See Photograph 9.1.

Vehicle Safety

As indispensable as the automobile has become to us, it attracts thieves, rapists and muggers, especially when the driver is alone.

Your best defense is to avoid dangerous situations. A woman, or man, alone in a stranded car can—and

9.1. Underside of a typical vehicle showing
various parts which a fleeing person can grab.

often does—attract unwanted company. To avoid being stranded make sure you always have plenty of fuel, and that your car is in good working condition. Find a good mechanic and have him/her check and tune-up your car every 3000 to 5000 miles. One way to find a reliable mechanic is through the automechanics teacher at your local high school or college. These teachers are usually very good mechanics themselves and are in a good position to recommend other reputable mechanics in your community.

When driving alone, stay on well-travelled freeways or roads as much as possible. You are more likely to get help quickly from police and other drivers if you are on a populated road. If harassed by another driver, don't take an unfamiliar off-ramp which may lead to an isolated area where you can be trapped.

Never pick up hitchhikers, especially if you are alone. Don't give strangers you meet in stores, restaurants, etc., a ride. Indeed, be cautious about talking with strangers you may meet in any public place. Don't give them information they can use against you, such as your address or the fact that you are travelling alone. Remain aloof and distant in your attitude toward the people you meet. You can do this while still being polite.

Double-check your car locks. They should be locked at all times. Pay particular attention to the lock on the passenger side. Sometimes a driver is attacked by unwanted passengers who have entered the car while it was stopped at a stop light. Some people have been dragged out of their unlocked vehicles and beaten to death.

Always carry change for emergency telephone calls in extra pockets, or in your glove compartment, as well as in your purse or wallet. If your purse is stolen, you will still have access to change in order to use a phone to summon help.

If you are being followed or harassed by another driver, drive to the nearest police, fire or well-lighted gas station. Never, under such circumstances, drive home. There have been numerous instances of robbers/rapists/batterers following victims all the way home from freeways or highways. Then as the victim walks from the car to an apartment or house, he or she is attacked.

Avoid carrying large amounts of cash with you. Rather, rely on credit cards, personal checks and traveler's checks. Keep a separate list of check and card numbers which you can give to the authorities should your purse, wallet or car be stolen.

While stopping at restaurants/hotels/motels never "flash" money, expensive-looking jewelry, or fancy clothing in public, especially when you are by yourself. The prosperous look draws the attention of thieves, muggers and rapists. In a major shopping mall in the middle of a Saturday afternoon, for example, a robber armed with a very sharp knife sliced off a victim's finger in order to get a $5,000.00 ring. The suspect got away with both the ring and the finger in spite of the presence of over 20 eye-witnesses including an armed private security guard who was frozen with shock.

On the other hand, we recommend you carry at least $20 with you at all times. Many robbers commit their crimes because they need money to buy drugs. If you have no cash, they may shoot you out of frustration.

If you are on a deserted road and you see someone who might be in trouble, don't get out of your car if you want to help. Rather, keep your car locked, the engine running and find out what the trouble is through a narrow opening in the window. Offer to drive to the nearest phone or service station to get help for them. Remember, it is very risky to give any stranger a ride.

If you see someone lying on the road—apparently hurt—don't get out of your car. He or she may be a decoy for hijackers, robbers, rapists or murderers. Immediately turn around and drive to the nearest phone and call the police or highway patrol.

When you park your car, lock it. Try to park it at the busiest and most well-lit part of the parking lot. When returning to your parked car be on the lookout for anyone lurking or loitering near your vehicle. Also, check your rear seat for any unwanted passengers before you open the door. If you see anything suspicious, go back to the store/theater/church and get help. You might want to review Chapter 5 for information about how to hold your keys as you approach your parked car.

Psychology

In the mid-1960s the nation was shocked by the murder of Kitty Genovese in New York City and the brutal rape of April Aaron in San Francisco. Ms. Genovese was repeatedly stabbed while nearly 40 eyewitnesses looked out their windows and did nothing to help her. Forensic experts believe that had anyone called the police during the first moments of her attack, officers would have arrived in time to save her life.

April Aaron was brutally attacked in front of over 20 eye-witnesses who did nothing to help her. Her attacker raped her in a public street and ended his attack by slashing her eyes with a knife rendering her permanently blind. Later he told authorities that he deliberately blinded her so she couldn't identify him in court. As it turned out she was able to accurately identify him non-visually anyway.

What seemed to shock the American public most was the fact that none of the bystanders did anything to help the victim—they didn't even call the police.

It is interesting to note that the presence of others may make it less likely that any one person will help. The results of Latane and Darley's studies of bystander behavior show that bystanders are more likely to help when alone than when in the presence of others.

Latane and Darley proposed the following three explanations for their observations:

1. *Audience Inhibition*: *We are slower to act in the presence of others out of fear of looking foolish in case there really is no emergency.*
2. **Social Influence**: *If everyone in a group of bystanders is trying to look calm and cool, the whole group may convince itself that there is no emer-*

gency.

3. <u>*Diffusion of Responsibility*</u>: *The sole bystander may feel that the responsibility to intervene is 100% his. And he or she, consequently, feels great pressure to help. With many bystanders, however, the burden of responsibility does not fall solely on one person and therefore the individual feels less pressure to intervene.*

Given these pressures against helping, we can be reasonably sure that if we are attacked we cannot rely on others to come to our aid. Even if well-meaning bystanders call the police on our behalf, it takes time for the police to respond. According to a recent FBI study, nationwide the average police response time in life-and-death situations is 16 minutes. Some jurisdictions react more quickly. LAPD's response time is, at times, as low as 2 minutes for such life-and-death calls as battery-in-progress, rape, armed robbery in progress, shots being fired, etc. But even 2 minutes is a very long time when you are under attack.

Whether we like it or not, therefore, the responsibility for our survival rests squarely on our own shoulders. Consequently the reader would be wise to review and regularly practice the contents of this book.

Chapter 9

Name:_____

Question 17

Discuss the impact of the presence of others in a helping situation.

Chapter 9

Name:_____

Describe and discuss the Latane and Darley research results.

Your Home

Home Security

By securing your home against burglars, vandals, or rapists, you can avoid spoiling an otherwise happy vacation or an uneventful day at work. A secure house/apartment also gives you peace of mind while you are gone, and when you return you are less likely to walk in on a burglar. Dead-bolt locks are recommended for the main doors. Sliding glass doors and windows can be secured by special locks. For recommended locks you can check with your local police department or with your local licensed locksmith.

If your community is burdened by very high burglary rates, you might consider installing decorative but solid iron bars on your doors and windows. For fire safety, be sure your grillwork can be opened from inside.

If you are away for any length of time, don't leave prowling burglars any clues about your absence. Depending on where you live, you should stop all deliveries including your mail. In some areas you can't trust the people responsible for regularly delivering items to your home. They may be in contact with professional burglars. We therefore recommend that you arrange with trusted neighbors or friends to pick up your delivered material (mail, newspapers, etc.) and appropriately store it for you. Also ask a friend or trusted neighbor to keep an eye on your home and to pick up any unexpected notes or samples of goods left at your door.

Leave lights on inside your house. It is especially good to leave the bathroom light on because the bathroom might be in use at any time during the day or night. Also leave the radio on to give the impression that someone is home.

Leave lights burning near the main entrances of the house. Burglars don't like to operate in the light. Leave extra lightbulbs with your trusted neighbor or friend and ask him/her to replace any that burn out.

Timers can increase the illusion that people are present and awake. One woman we know has a living room light on a timer so that a reading chair is lit between 11 and 2 a.m. and then again between 4 and 5:30 a.m. Burglars and attackers tend to avoid insomniacs.

Get a house-sitter if you plan to be away for any length of time. An occupied house is a less vulnerable target for burglars and vandals. Also, an unkempt lawn or garden may provide the burglars with clues about your absence. Therefore have someone you trust look after your yard while you are away.

Inform your local police about your absence and give them a list of the names of people you have authorized to enter your premises. If there is an ongoing neighborhood watch program in your area inform them also.

Drain and cover your pool, if you have one. Pools attract uninvited children who may hurt themselves in and around the pool or elsewhere on your property. Unless you take reasonable safety precautions, you can be legally liable for any accidents which may occur on your property.

If your neighborhood has been plagued by burglaries and vandalism, get together with your neighbors to organize a neighborhood watch with the help of your local police. Ms. Esta Yonce, Crime Prevention Specialist (ret.) in the Los Angeles Police Department's West Valley Area, reports that an ongoing, active neighborhood watch is one of the most effective ways of stopping all kinds of crime including burglary. In fact, such neighborhood watch activities typically have the immediate effect of reducing burglaries by an average of 40%.

Never be too embarrassed or uncomfortable to call the police if you see anything or anyone that seems suspicious to you. For instance individuals trying different doors of houses or cars could also be burglars or thieves.

Door-to-door salesmen may not be legitimate. Don't

let them into your house or apartment. Install a peep-hole which allows you to see who is outside without opening the door and risking attack. If anyone at your door tries to force it open, immediately call the police. Dial 911 and let the dispatcher know that someone is in the process of forcing an entry. We recommend using telephones which have memory capacity for certain numbers. Emergency numbers can be pre-programmed so that during life-and-death emergencies you just need to push one button to reach the appropriate number.

Do not enter your home, even after a brief absence, if something-anything-doesn't look right. The door(s) might be ajar, or as you look in you might see that your place has been ransacked. Immediately leave, run to your neighbor's house or apartment and call the police from there. Don't risk walking in on a dangerous burglar and getting yourself injured or killed. We know about one elderly gentleman who came home from a movie to find his apartment door open, walked in and confronted a young burglar. The burglar picked up a wooden chair, broke off one of its legs and beat the man so severely that he spent 4 weeks in the hospital. The victim died 7 months later. We therefore recommend waiting for the police to search your place before you enter it.

Psychology

According to police data most burglars are drug addicts who need to get in and out of a victim's home as quickly as possible. Any delay caused by sturdy locks, dogs, people, etc., means a delay in getting the drug which the addict/burglar needs. He will therefore choose only the most vulnerable residences to burglarize.

Addiction can be described as physical dependence or psychological dependence. According to Hilgard et al., physical dependence is characterized by:

1. *Tolerance. The user must take more and more of the drug to get the same effect.*

2. *Withdrawal. Discontinuing use of the drug is followed by unpleasant/painful physical symptoms.*

Psychological dependence is a learned need for the drug through repeated use. If you habitually use a drug to relieve anxiety, for instance, you may feel you need it even if there is no physical dependence.

Cocaine, especially in the form of "crack", is extremely addictive and can very quickly get you hooked. For example, a very successful, high-income manager of a major Los Angeles business went to a party where he was introduced to cocaine by a friend. Within 9 months the manager was arrested by the police for embezzling his employer. His huge salary was not enough to support both his habit and his family.

Heroin addicts still make up a large portion of the addict/burglary population. These addicts seem to be both psychologically and physically dependent.

Psychologically, heroin produces changes in mood and self-confidence and reduces anxiety. Youths report that on heroin they forget all their troubles. Experienced adult users report an intensely pleasurable "rush" within a couple of minutes after mainlining (i.e., injecting heroin directly into a vein). This "rush" according to some is similar to an orgasm. It's important to beware of drugs. Drug use changes the body's chemistry and can seriously impair its ability to experience pleasure without the artificial assistance of the substance.

Physically, heroin dependence can develop very quickly. Tolerance is rapid and withdrawal is very intense. Consequently, users often risk overdosage in order to get the high they desire. Withdrawal includes chills, sweating, stomach cramps, vomiting and headaches. The heroin addict needs to use the drug every 5-7 hours to avoid withdrawal symptoms which leaves him or her very little time to burglarize your home. These addicts, therefore, tend to choose easy victims.

Chapter 10

Name:_____

Question 19
Discuss addiction and its consequences.

Chapter 10

Name:_____

Question 20
Describe the role of drug addiction in burglary.

Child Safety

Safety In The Home

Approximately 3500 children under the age of 5 die by accident each year. A touch over 4000 children between the age of 5 and 15 die accidentally each year. In other words the accidental deaths of children in the U.S., hovers around 7500 each year. About 1000 of the under-5 infants die in car accidents, 800 by drowning, roughly 300 through ingestion, about 200 are poisoned, close to 1000 are burned, about 150 fall to their deaths, and about 50 die via firearms. Between 60% and 70% of these children are boys and the vast majority of these accidents occur in or around the victim's home.

The average home is so full of hazards for children—especially small children—that the safest rule to follow is never to leave children unattended. Children can exercise incredible ingenuity in finding dangerous material to play with. Responsible adult intervention is therefore often necessary.

Your medicine cabinet, for instance, probably has

dangerous poisons and cutting instruments which fascinate your youngsters. Be sure such cabinets are out of the reach of small children. The medicine cabinets should have difficult to open doors which curious youngsters cannot open. Medicine and poisons should be kept in the newer type of childproof containers. These containers have special lids which must be positioned in a particular way before they can be removed. Children (and some adults) have great difficulty opening such containers.

If there are stairs in your house, you can prevent small children from climbing them by placing barriers across them. You can use a piece of large flat board across the top of stairs to block children from climbing or falling. Wooden folding gates are also available from children's stores. Carpeting on your stairs helps cushion any accidental fall.

Keep sharp instruments/tools away from children. Tweezers, paper clips, scissors, knives, needles, forks, etc., are all potential hazards. Such items should be placed in cabinets or drawers which are either out of your child's reach or securely locked against an attempt to get into them. A series of drawers with loop-type handles can be easily secured by placing a stick through all the handles simultaneously. Knobbed drawers or handles can be somewhat secured by using plastic strips with slits through which the knobs can be pushed. In these ways the attempt to open one drawer means pulling against the others as well, making it difficult to open any of them. Check at your local market for other childproof safety devices.

Don't leave unsafe electric cords lying around. It's quite easy for a child to plug one end into an outlet and electrocute him/herself on the other end. Make sure all appliances are either turned off or placed out of reach so the youngsters can't burn themselves.

Never leave children unattended near a swimming pool and always abide by the rules that should be posted near the pool. A life saver (or any floating, safety item) should also be handy in case of an emergency. Drained pools should be completely covered with (semi-) solid material to prevent anyone from falling in. Fence your pool area whenever possible to keep out neighboring youngsters who want to use it without your knowledge. Many communities have ordinances which legally require you to enclose your pool.

Don't leave seldom or unused refrigerators standing around without removing the locking devices. Better still, remove the doors completely. All too often children have playfully locked themselves into such iceboxes and suffocated to death.

If you have an accident or medical emergency, call the Fire/Sheriff/Police Department's paramedic unit. For ready access to emergency numbers list them and keep copies of the list near your telephones as well as in your car. In an emergency you can dial 911 (or O for operator) to get the appropriate help. Also be sure that your children and other household members (including the babysitter) know how to call for emergency assistance should the need arise.

Although only about 50 infants die each year because of firearm accidents (a small number compared with other causes of accidental deaths), this type of accident is particularly vexing because it is so easily preventable. Don't just tell your children not to touch any firearms you may have in your house because firearms hold too strong an attraction for youngsters to merely respond to such directives. Instead exercise other, more effective options.

If you have children, you may want to get rid of your guns until your kids are mature enough to be educated in gun safety. However, given the high crime rates in many areas, you may opt to keep guns in the house for protection. There are trigger-guard locks or special gun cabinets you can buy to render the firearms safe from children. Check with the local chapter of the National Rifle Association or a nearby, reputable gun dealer for more detailed information about such security items.

Child Molesting

Child molesting is one of the major problems experienced by children and their families. The molester's impact upon the child can vary from being mild to very extreme depending on the actual act of molestation as well as on the reactions of the people around the victim. There is no known way to identify a child molester until he or she actually begins to molest children. The molester looks like anyone you might know and trust. Like rapists, molesters are often family members who frequently enjoy good relations with their own sons and daughters. Often the child has previously been acquainted with the offender. The majority of the victims are under 8 years of age, but some of them are as old as 16.

About one-sixth of the victims resist and tell their parents. But others, perhaps due to lack of appropriate attention at home, keep returning to the offender. Children have strong love, attention and affectional needs. If these needs are not reasonably met at home, the youngsters will be receptive to such attention coming from outside the home. Molesters are very good at picking victims who are emotionally hungry. They use the child's needs to manipulate the child into cooperating with them. Children in stable, loving homes tend to have greater emotional security to resist/survive molestations with less psychological trauma.

The actual molestation can sometimes have a less disturbing impact upon the child than the reactions of people after the incident(s). Parents, relatives, and friends should remain calm and warm. Home life should continue as normally as possible, and the child should be helped, as much as possible, to understand the experience and why it might have happened. Try to help the victim feel accepted and loved in order to survive the molestation with a minimum of long-term, mental/emotional damage. Above all be cognizant of the fact that the molestation is not the child's fault. The victim is completely free of culpability but by your behavior/attitude may feel guilty and responsible which can lead to mental problems.

Teach your children as early as possible safety precautions to minimize the risk of being molested. Local police departments, social service agencies and schools/colleges often offer safety classes. Call your local agency for the times and locations of these classes.

For example, teach your children to never accept automobile rides from strangers. The youngster should be taught to keep his or her distance from a stranger's car while giving directions or to avoid giving directions entirely. You can have your child point strangers to a gas station or store for directions. If someone tries to force the child into a vehicle, screaming and running toward the nearest populated area is a recommended strategy.

If the child is active in selling such items as Girl

Scout cookies, lemonade, magazines, etc., s/he should be accompanied by others. Halloween trick-or-treating should also be done in groups accompanied by adults. Furthermore the treats should be carefully examined. There have been incidences where food items contained needles, tacks and razor blades.

Children should be taught to never play near public restrooms, back alleys or any desolate place. Neither should they take short cuts through or past such places. When going to movie theaters, they should go in groups. Teach them to report anyone attempting to touch them inappropriately to the theater manager or usher.

It is also very important to teach your children never to let anyone into the home when they are alone. As soon as the youngster is old enough, teach him/her to dial 911 (or O for operator) to get emergency help. When parents are out of the house, they should always leave phone numbers where they can be reached by the children or their babysitters.

Instruct babysitters never to let the children out of their sight. Nor should babysitters allow their friends into the house except with the clear permission of the child's parents. Instruct babysitters not to allow strangers into the house regardless of the plausible-sounding reasons such strangers may give. Furthermore, the babysitter should always be left with phone numbers where parents can be reached.

Choose babysitters with the greatest of care. If the sitter is a stranger to you, get references and check them out thoroughly. An irresponsible sitter can bring tragedy into your home. Babysitters have been known to expose their employers and wards to molesters, drugs, kidnappers, burglars and dangerous neglect.

Psychology

Child molestation is a major concern of many parents. According to Coleman, Butcher and Carson, most pedophiliacs* are men, although women also occasionally molest children. The definition of adult versus child can vary from state to state, country to country, and culture to culture. Some countries/cultures make no, or few, distinctions between children and adults with respect to sex (e.g., France). Contact with the victim usually involves fondling the genitals. At times the child is manipulated into fondling the pedophiliac's sex organ or into mouth-genital contacts. It is relatively rare for the pedophiliac to attempt coitus.

The work of Revitch and Weiss suggests that older molesters prefer immature children and younger offenders seek adolescent girls 12-15 years of age. There are about twice as many female as there are male victims.

---

*Pedophilia is a condition in which an adult wishes to have, or actually has, sex with children.

The offender usually knows the victim, and the sexual behavior may continue over time. Usually physical force is not used. Swanson found that only 3 out of the 25 cases he studied involved the active participation of the victim.

The reader should be cautioned about having too much faith in these data because most researchers end up with a **convenience** or incidental sample of people for their study. Such samples are risky in the sense that they may not be representative of the population of victims we might be interested in. Sgroi, for example, makes the point that many cases of sexual assaults on youngsters probably go unreported because the parents want to protect the child against further ordeal.

Cohen, Seghorn and Calmas found that the most common type of pedophiliac is one who was not able to have satisfactory interpersonal relationships with peers throughout his life. Sexually he is comfortable only with children and usually knows the victim.

A less common type is the man who has feelings of masculine inadequacy and responds to rejection by his spouse or girlfriend by molesting immature girls, often strangers.

Another common type of child molester is the pedophiliac whose primary aim is aggression. These are hostile psychopaths who often injure the child.

Regardless of the type of offender, prevention by

carefully observing adults who interact with your children and stopping any relationships which look suspicious is, unfortunately, a necessary part of modern parenthood.

Chapter 11

Name:_____

Question 21
Briefly discuss child molestation.

Chapter 11

Name:_____

Question 22
Describe the different types of pedophiliacs.

Domestic Violence

Introduction

Domestic violence and abuse is found in families from all walks of life—rich and poor as well as every known ethnic and religious group. Sometimes adults batter children and sometimes adults physically abuse their elderly parents. In fact according to a Congressional report, one in 25 elderly adults is abused. Every other woman will be struck by her partner some time during her life. Approximately 40% of all murdered women are killed by their husbands or partners.

Although the vast majority of domestic violence victims are women, men are sometimes the victims of their wives. In Los Angeles, for example, a wife encouraged her husband to drink excessive amounts of alcohol until he passed out. She then repeatedly struck him with a baseball bat. He spent two weeks in a coma and needed over a year to recover enough to work again. In New York City a woman beat her wheelchair-bound husband to death by using a hammer on him over a period of several months. However, over 95% of the abuse among heterosexual couples involves male batterers and female victims.

In fact, about 4000 women are beaten to death annually. This statistic combined with the non-fatal cases means that in the United States every 15 seconds a woman is physically assaulted within her home. (Compiled by Ruth Peachey, M.D., 1989.) There are more victims of battery than AIDS victims. Nine out of 10 murdered women are murdered by men, four out of five are murdered in their home and almost three out of four are murdered by husbands or lovers.

Legal Definitions

Throughout the United States the legal descriptions of domestic violence and abuse (as well as their components) are being more clearly and specifically defined. In California, for example, **domestic violence** is defined as follows (from various California Penal Code sections including 240, 242, 245, 261, 273, 415, 594, 603, 653, 13700, etc.):

...(It)is **abuse committed against an adult or fully emancipated minor** who is a spouse, former spouse, cohabitant, former cohabitant, or a person with whom the suspect has had a child or has or had a dating or engagement relationship.

Abuse, in turn, is defined as:

...intentionally or recklessly causing or attempting to cause bodily injury, or placing another person in reasonable apprehension of imminent serious bodily injury to himself or another.

The legal definition of cohabitant is:

...two or more persons who presently live or reside in the same household or who have in the past lived or resided in the same household irrespective of whether they are, or have been in the past, involved in a sexual relationship.

The California Penal Code Section 273.5 further describes the felonious consequence of corporal injury as follows:

Any person who willfully inflicts upon his or her spouse, or any person who willfully inflicts upon any person of the opposite sex with whom he or she is cohabiting, or any person who willfully inflicts upon any person who is the mother or father of his or her child, corporal injury resulting in a traumatic condition, is guilty of a felony.

As used in this section, "traumatic condition" means a condition of the body, such as a wound or external or internal injury, whether of a minor or serious nature, caused by physical force. These detailed legal definitions were, in part, necessitated by the over 5000 calls per month to battery hotlines in Los Angeles County alone.

What The Victim Can Do

If you are battered, you can call the police. More and more states and individual police departments are becoming enlightened about the need to protect and safeguard domestic violence victims. In California, for example, wife beating is a crime and depending on the extent of injury, the police can make a felony arrest. If you are afraid that the batterer may return to hurt you, you can ask the police to issue an Emergency Restraining Order.

In order to implement the Emergency Restraining Order the police will call a judge and explain your situation to him. The judge can approve the issue which is then good until the end of the next court day. This gives you time to obtain a permanent court order. If the batterer violates the restraining order, the police will arrest him.

There are a growing number of organizations specifically geared to help you with legal, economic and psychological counsel. We recommend calling them whether or not you have already called the police. In fact, we recommend calling them even if you have not been physically abused. If you have any fears or suspicions about your domestic life, call these organizations in order to avoid deterioration in your family's relationships.

National Coalition Against Domestic Violence, PO Box 15127, Washington, DC. 20003-0127, Ph. 800-333-SAFE.

Southern California Coalition On Battered Women, PO Box 5036, Santa Monica, California. 90405. Ph. (310) 392-9874.

Elder Abuse Hotline, 800- 992-1660,

Child Abuse Hotline for which you dial "O" and ask for Zenith 2-1234.

If the batterer is not in police custody, and he continues to be a threat to you and your children, you can go to a shelter. Shelters are houses that temporarily provide a safe place for battered women and their youngsters. The location of these houses are kept secret so that he can't find you. For access to shelters call any of the above hotline numbers.

Psychology

Batterers' Profiles

Although family battery occurs in virtually any type of household, various studies of batterers indicate a fairly consistent profile with respect to the typical batterer.

Batterers tend to blame others for their own behavior. They reject responsibility for their unacceptable/illegal activity. "She asked for it," or "she provoked me," or "it's her fault," are not uncommon statements made by batterers. They refuse to see the victim as not wanting to be hurt.

Men who batter allow their anger to be expressed through direct aggression and violence as though a direct "line" links their feelings of anger with physical/verbal/manipulative abuse. It is as though batterers have never learned alternate and acceptable strategies for expressing their anger.

Jealousy is another part of the batterer's profile, especially when it is extreme or pathological. The batterer may go to great lengths and expense to "spy" on the victim for no reality-based reasons. He often has strong fears that the victim will leave, and his low self-esteem makes it difficult for him to accept the notion that she might want to be independent of him.

Traditional gender role and a violent family background are also often found within the batterer's immediate family. In fact about 90% of batterers come from violent families in which the values of a dominant, bread-winning father and submissive, domestic mother were strongly accepted. Often such families imply, or overtly express, beliefs that forcible behavior is good for the family.

In fact, the belief that it is okay to use force is associated with spousal rape. Recent years have seen more and more use of sex to express aggression. Although many unenlightened people still believe that men have the "right" to their wives or girlfriends and that the victim does not have the right to say "no" when she wants to, in most states marital rape is a crime. The reader is referred to Chapters 2 & 3 for information about rape.

One final component to the batterer's profile is substance abuse. Approximately 65% of the battery incidents reported to the police involve alcohol. Experts tend to agree that alcohol reduces whatever inhibitions the abuser may have. This makes it easier for him to lose control of himself and to attack his victim.

The above profile is not complete because there are batterers out there who don't seem to "fit." However, if you are a woman whose husband or boyfriend has any or all of these profile-aspects, you might seriously consider calling a local hotline for advice. The trained personnel working these lines can often help you prevent potential problems from escalating toward dangerous levels.

Cycles Of Battering

Experts describe battery in terms of three phases or cycles: Romantic love, tension building, battering. If the couple is still together at the end of the third phase, the relationship usually goes back to the love phase which tempts the victim to forgive the batterer and stay with him. If she stays with him these cycles increase in frequency, and the abuse becomes more and more severe as the cycle repeats itself.

The love stage is perceived as very romantic by both of them. They make up and the batterer becomes charming and manipulative. He expresses the belief that his anger can be controlled and that he will never abuse her again. He expresses strong emotional dependency on her "...can't live without you," and showers her with gifts and attention. The victim begins to feel responsible for the batterer's actions and her own victimization.

The tension building stage is marked by increasing anger in the batterer which the victim denies and believes to be controllable even though she can sense his edginess. Both find themselves unable to openly discuss the underlying problem of his anger. The batterer becomes verbally abusive, reducing her to an object— one that is okay to beat. And she comes to feel that the battering is deserved.

The third, or battering, stage is marked by tension building to the point where the suspect loses control and batters. The battery may begin with a push or shove but eventually escalates to slaps, kicks and punches. Then there can be further escalation onto the use of weapons and more serious injuries. The batterer usually claims that he doesn't want to hurt the victim but merely to teach her a lesson. He is usually very good at rationalizing his actions and blames her for them. And both he and the victim tend to minimize the seriousness of the injuries. As the victim accepts the blame, the cycle begins again with the love phase which is the "carrot" which induces both to stay together.

Chapter 12

Name:_____

Compare any aspect(s) of the batterer's profile with a real-life batterer you are acquainted with.

Chapter 12

Name:_____

Question 24

Very briefly describe the Cycles Of Battery and, using your imagination, suggest ways of breaking the cycle.

CHAPTER 13

Taste:

A Theory of Survival*

A True Life Scenario

Two police officers were on routine patrol. A citizen waved his arms at them desperately trying to get their attention. They drove a block past him, made a U-turn and slowly rolled back toward him. They did this in order to visually inspect the whole environment just in case they were being set up to be assassinated. Everything looked normal so they allowed the citizen to approach the black & white making sure they could see his hands—after all it's the hands that typically kill police officers.

The citizen informed the officers that he saw the rear glass door of an otherwise locked business smashed. The officers drove to the back alley where they noted

We owe a debt of gratitude to LAPD officer Jerry Mulford (Ret.) for significant contributions to the concepts contained in this chapter. This extremely intelligent and perceptive police officer was the first professional to alert us, supraliminally, to taste.

the broken door.

They called for backup and a field supervisor. When these arrived, the officers entered the structure with their guns in one hand and flashlights in the other. There was no electricity in the place.

They tactically did a zone to zone search, taking turns clicking the flashlights on & off and sidestepping. The place seemed clear.

All of a sudden one of the officers felt a bitter taste in his mouth. At a recent law enforcement conference he heard that this taste can be a warning of danger, so he decided on a bluff.

Although he couldn't see anything he yelled into the darkness, "all right you, I see you, come on out hands first–I want to see your hands...NOW."

After a brief pause the officers heard a man's voice, "O.K., I'm coming out, I'm coming out."

The flashlights clicked on and emerging from a hiding place the light revealed two hands—one holding a large wrench.

There are a growing number of anecdotes describing how taste gives us clues about imminent danger. These experiences involving both police officers and civilians, raise the question of how taste and subliminal perception are related. We invite any of our readers with such experiences to write them down and mail them to us.

Subliminal Perception

Within the scientific community anecdotes are considered to be very weak evidence.

More rigorous scientific studies show that the phenomenon of subliminal perception exists in the sense that we can unconsciously detect lights, sounds, odors, etc., which are not sufficiently intense for us to be aware of them. However, our brains still process these low intensity signals and, in response, our emotions and our bodies can be affected.

Anecdotal experiences such as the one described in the above section, together with the scientific findings, suggest that danger signals can indeed be unconsciously picked up, processed by the brain and translated into that bitter taste.

Theory

We submit the proposition that subliminal perception (see footnote on next page) of a predator's sounds, body odors, etc., can be translated into a bitter taste in one's mouth.

Sounds include those based on breathing, heartbeat, body leaning against something, etc.

There is some evidence that our body odors reflect

emotions. When we are angry at someone our bodies emit a slightly different odor than when we are friendly. When we are about to (counter)attack our bodies give forth yet another odor.

Thus, for instance, the police officer in the opening section of this chapter could have subliminally** picked up information from the hidden suspect as follows:

–the suspect's body odor is that of a predator.

–the suspect's breathing:

—changes in air pressure due to his breathing,

—the subliminal sound of breathing.

–the sound of the suspect's small movements while leaning against a wall/barrier.

Millions of years' of evolution have programmed into the police officer's natural defensive system(s) the capacity to translate these subliminal sensory experiences into the telltale bitter taste.

Our ancestors, after all, had to rely heavily on their sense of taste (among other things) for their survival. Without taste they could not, for instance detect poisonous or spoiled food. It is, therefore, reasonable to deduce that taste as an early warning danger signal has been inherited by us from our evolutionary past.

**The word subliminal is a combination of the English 'sub' meaning below and the Latin 'limen' meaning threshold. In the term *subliminal perception* the term 'subliminal' refers to sensory experiences occurring below our conscious awareness but which the brain still processes and to which we can still respond in some way, e.g., bitter taste.

Other Applications

"Listening" to one's taste can, we submit, alert us to danger giving us the opportunity to avoid it. So far we are relying on mere anecdotes, however, future scientific works may well support these.

A Date Rape Example

A young lady, who had just heard about this taste theory at a crime prevention seminar, was "picked up" by a man she was attracted to at a party.

He offered to drive her home and she consented. On the way she suddenly felt a bitter taste in her mouth. Upon arrival she immediately let him know with firmness in her voice that the evening was over. Sensing her firmness he politely left. Several weeks later she discovered that this same young man was arrested for date rape and aggravated assault.

Avoiding A Setup

A young man met an attractive woman, in town on a business trip, at a nightclub. They hit it off very well and she invited him to her hotel room.

On the way he got an uncomfortable bitter taste in his mouth. Having recently heard about this as a possible warning signal, he decided to not go into her room, shook her hand and said good-bye to her.

A month later he was shocked to read in the newspaper about that woman and her husband being arrested for forced sodomy and oral copulation. She lured male victims to her hotel room where she held a gun on them while her husband sexually assaulted them.

Preventing Legal Abuse

A young male college student was strongly attracted to a coed, and she seemed very responsive and seductive. They attended a couple of social events and decided to be sexually active.

Just prior to what would have been their first sexual encounter they met on campus and she suggested going to her apartment. At this moment he noticed a bitter taste in his mouth. Having recently heard about this taste theory of self defense, he decided not to go with her.

The following semester he heard that she claimed that she was date raped accusing another student of committing the rape.

Detailed investigation cleared the accused. Further investigation revealed that one year prior to this incident the same coed at another college in another state was actually charged with filing a false police report when her claims of date rape were shown to be false.

The above examples are among a growing number of anecdotes supporting our theory that taste plays a major role in survival.

Psychology

The systematic study of sensation and perception was begun even before Wundt's, 1879 Leipzig laboratory. The pioneers include the German physiologist Ernst Weber (1795-1878) and physicist and experimental psychologist Gustav Fechner (1801-1887).

These pioneers began the study of **psychophysics** which is a precursor of modern Engineering Psychology.

Psychophysics is the study of the relationship between the physical energy of stimuli and the psychological experience of those stimuli. That is, to what extent does your subjective experience of, for instance, the brightness of a lamp match its actual, measurable brightness.

Psychophycisists deal with such sensory concepts as *Reizlimen* and *Differential Limen.*

Reizlimen

Reizlimen, also known as RL or Absolute Threshold, is, in general, the minimum intensity a stimulus must be before you are aware of its presence.

This refers to how bright a light must be before you notice it. Or, how loud a sound is before you are conscious of it.

Differential Limen

Differential Limen, also known as DL or Difference Threshold, is, in general, the smallest difference in the magnitude of two stimuli that you can consciously detect.

This refers to how different the brightnesses of two lights must be before you notice that there is a difference. Or, how different the loudnesses between two sources of sound must be before you are conscious of the difference.

j.n.d., or just noticeable difference is a technical term often used to describe the minimum difference between the intensities of two sources of stimuli which you are barely aware of.

Subliminal Perception

As mentioned before in this chapter subliminal perception refers to stimulus intensities, _below_ Absolute Thresholds, being processed by our brains such that our behaviors (e.g., bitter taste) are influenced by them.

For further inquiry the reader is referred to samples of studies in this area (Balay, J., & Shevrin, H., 1988; Dixon, N. F., 1971; Duncan, J., 1985; Krosnick, J. A., Jussim, L. J., & Lynn, A. R., 1992; Silverman, L.H., 1983) which support the possibility of subliminal perception.

Weber's Law

In 1834 Ernst Weber discovered the first principle of sensation which today is known as Weber's Law or Weber's Ratio.

Weber's law states that the smallest detectable difference in stimulus energy (i.e., j.n.d.) is a constant fraction (i.e., ratio) of the intensity of the stimulus.

Weber's law can be algebraically presented as,

$$k = \Delta I / I$$

k, here, means a constant value,
ΔI is the same as j.n.d.,
I is the intensity of a stimulus.

Suppose you just notice a difference between two lights when one is at 60 watts and the other is at 62 watts. That is, ΔI is equal to 2 and I equals 60. Using the above Weber formula your k value is 1/30.

This, in turn, means that when you begin with both sources of light being at 120 you would notice the difference when one is 124. That is, 4/120, or that constant, k, of 1/30.

It turns out that when engineering psychologists are designing man-machine systems (e.g., automobiles) for the average person, the Weber function works pretty well. However, for extreme stimulus intensities, it doesn't work.

Thus when we're designing equipment, say for outer space or under water work where the astronauts or scuba divers at times work under conditions involving extreme stimulus intensities, Weber's Law is not as useful.

Astronauts, for example, at times have to use equipment under very bright or very dim illumination. At other times it is very hot or very cold for them. Then we have extreme variations of pressure, etc. For designing human operated equipment for such conditions we must turn to some of Fechner's work.

Fechner

Gustav Fechner pioneered the development of variations of the Weber Function while he was continuing to find out how the mind responds to external reality.

One major insight Fechner had was that the senses did not notice the absolute differences between stimuli, but rather their relative intensity.

Thus, when danger is approaching, the important thing to know is how rapidly it is approaching, that is, how much louder one threatening sound is than another, and not the absolute volume of any given sound.

Fechner developed a whole family of algebraic formulae variations of which are still being used by modern engineering psychologists or human factors engineers. These formulae are collectively called Weber-

Fechner functions. An example of such a formula is,

$$S = k \log I$$

which reads S equals k multiplied by the logarithm of I. S refers to perceived sensory differences, k is the Weber constant, and logI is the logarithm of intensity.

Although Weber and Fechner worked in the 19th century, they laid the groundwork for the design of complex man-machine-computer systems of the 21st century.

13.1. Typical LAPD police unit manned by Bernie Weiss and partner Ofcr. Linda Crispin.

Taste: A Theory of Survival

Chapter 13

Name:_____

Question 25

Discuss the differences and similarities of Weber's Law and the Weber-Fechner functions.

Chapter 13

Name:_____

Question 26
Discuss the role taste might have had for our ancestors' survival.

Body Language

Our Bodies and Self Defense

Posture

The good news is that not everyone gets assaulted. But that leaves several questions. For example, how does an assailant choose who to pursue, pick on or physically attack? Another, even more important question is, how can you avoid being chosen?

Unfortunately, there is no safety pill or perfect system for self protection. But research shows that your body signals and the psychology behind them are a strong deterrent to attackers.

According to Joan Nelson (Self Defense, Steps to Success, 1991), one of the best ways to resist being selected as a victim is to "project an un-victimlike, confident and vigilant demeanor." The Queen's Bench Foundation's Project Rape Response (U.S. Dept. of Justice, 1976) found that "physical appearance or assertive body language" tended to exclude a woman from potential attack.

Criminals themselves tell us they look for people who are looking down. This is such a common attribute of mugging victims that psychologists have labeled it the "downcast demeanor". If a person acts distracted, with behavior such as brooding, staring at the sidewalk, searching through a purse or bag, or reading a map, Joel Kirsch (Los Angeles Police Dept. Consultant) found they were more likely to be attacked. Another cue that assailants seem to notice is head and eye movement. People with exaggerated or furtive eye movements or sweeping side-to-side head movements—which may imply fear, preoccupation, or being off guard—are more likely to be assaulted.

In contrast to the downcast demeanor, people of royal heritage are described as holding their chins high. "A lady never bows," is the way one elderly woman described appropriate street behavior from her grandmother's era (about 1870) in Atlanta, Georgia. This is good self defense training for both men and women today.

Typically in upper middle class homes, children are taught to sit and stand up straight because that is correct and appropriate behavior. Slouching or slumping are habits associated with lower status or position in life. Indeed, we call someone a "slouch" when we want to imply that they are awkward, lazy or inept.

Likewise, a slumping posture is associated with low energy, poor body coordination, and low self-esteem.

John T. Molloy, of "Dress for Success" fame, has found that "upper-middle-class people walk, stand, sit, and hold their heads at different angles than lower-middle-class people" (Molloy's Live for Success, 1981) They even use and hold their facial muscles differently. Furthermore, his research shows "if you avoid the mannerisms of lower-socioeconomic groups and emulate those of the upper-socioeconomic groups, you will receive better treatment in this world."

In his research, he had men and women in singles bars judge the other people in the bar, including an actor and actress playing different "posture" roles.

The women who judged the "actor" responded very differently depending on whether he stood and walked in a straight, upper-middle-class type posture or had his shoulders hunched in a more lower-middle-class posture. In reality, the young man was 5 feet, 10 inches tall and weighed 143 pounds. When he slumped, he lost 7 pounds and 1 inch (to 5'9" and 136 pounds), and was described as "sheepish and ineffective". When he stood up straight, the women guessed him to be 5 feet 11+ inches and 160 pounds. (He gained 17 pounds and more than an inch in height.) Better yet, the women described him as "virile and manly".

On a rating scale of 1 to 10 with 10 being the highest

score, a slumped posture for the actor brought him a score of 4; with an erect posture he rated an 8. The actress, standing erect in an upper-middle-class posture scored a 9.

Additional support for a straight posture comes from research at the University of Helsinki, Finland, where taller women were found to convey more authority. Likewise research by Pauline Bart (Stopping Rape, 1988) showed that women who were able to avoid being raped by an attacker were more likely to be taller.

Although you can't increase your height, standing with a straight posture can give you a taller appearance. And, overall, Molloy points out that when you have an erect, upper-middle-class body posture, other people, regardless of their background, find you more beautiful, intelligent and competent all of which are likely to deter an attacker.

In addition to an upright posture, you may want to practice projecting power in order to control a potentially threatening situation. Police officers, for example, are trained to exude an image of power and authority in order to control criminals. Molloy describes the basic authority stance as "almost military in nature: the shoulders squared, the head erect, the jaw muscles tight, the mouth closed and unsmiling, feet planted firmly on the floor and eyes steady."

It's important not to lose your power image when

you open you mouth. In general the lower the pitch of your voice, the more power and authority your voice brings you. Molloy suggests that 95 percent of both men and women can increase their image of power and authority by dropping their voices a half to a full octave. This is particularly important in self defense. A fast, high-pitched voice makes you sound fearful, helpless. Using a firm, deep sounding voice on the other hand, brings you into control.

Molloy points out that the "order-giving voices of some of the best women power figures in business are steely, icy, precise and distinct." When you tell a potential attacker, "leave me alone", remember the sound of crisis success and *use an order giving tone.*

Body Language

Betty Grayson (1978 Dissertation) is another researcher who has contributed directly to understanding the body language cues that criminals use in selecting a victim.

On an ordinary day in New York City, Grayson came up the subway stairwell, stepped onto the sidewalk, and was mugged. When she reported the incident to the police, they mentioned that attacks at that location were common. For Grayson, this was just enough information to turn her experience into a research project for her dissertation in sociology. What was the nonverbal behavior that caused some people to be attacked and not others?

From an opposite building, Betty filmed people coming out of the subway—old people, young people, mothers with children, business executives, salespeople. Some were assaulted, some were not. Then she cut and spliced the film removing the attackers, so it only showed people stepping onto the sidewalk and walking away.

Next, she showed the film to criminals in jail for assault and asked them to select the individuals *they* would have attacked. Sure enough, they picked the people who *had been* assaulted. Surprisingly, they often chose a younger or bigger person over an older or smaller individual. But they couldn't explain what they were looking for or why they chose one victim instead of another. Grayson, still curious about what signals made some people more desirable as potential victims, took the film to dancers, recognizing that they were movement experts. Their lab analysis pinpointed distinct body motions that were repeatedly demonstrated by those who had been attacked. These movements were not associated with age or gender, but they were associated with assault.

Here's what Grayson found and what we can learn about safe versus dangerous body signals:

1. *Those people who walked flat-footed instead of*

heel-to-toe were likely to be attacked. So, for safety, don't shuffle or plod, no matter how tired, sick or discouraged you might be. Instead, put your heel down first, distinctly and firmly.

2. Exaggerated strides—either too long or too short—attracted attackers. The length of your stride should approximate the width of your shoulders. In this way, you balance your walk to your height. Kirsch also found that walking speed—faster or slower than traffic—attracts attention from criminals. Both speeds may be associated with distraction, which (as mentioned earlier) is one of the attributes criminals observe from people's faces when choosing a victim. Matching your stride to others around you is a good way to deter attackers.

3. Swinging the same side arm and leg when stepping was another cue that attackers selected. By stepping forward with your left leg and left arm at the same time, you cause lateral motion in your body which creates an awkward, unbalanced impression, encouraging an assailant to think that you are less likely or able to defend yourself. On the other hand, if you swing your opposite arm as you step, you present a more balanced and self-directed image.

The benefits of opposite arm and leg movement have

been corroborated by child development studies. Specifically, research shows that children who crawl with the same side arm and leg movement will not only be more clumsy in sports and general body motion, but will also have difficulty learning to read, even to the point of being dyslexic. By relearning how to crawl with opposite side arm and leg movements, children have been able to dramatically improve their reading and learning skills.

The value of opposite side arm and leg movement is connected with the structure of the brain. The right side of the brain governs movement on the left side of the body and vice versa. This means that when you swing the left arm and step with the right leg you use both sides of your brain. Thus you get more brain exercise with opposite side leg and arm movement. In the tradition of use it or lose it, a more active brain translates into higher intelligence, more skill, and overall greater ability to live successfully, all of which are subtle deterrents to attackers.

4. Attackers chose people whose upper body seemed to move in a different direction than their lower body. (This is sometimes called the "John Wayne" walk because the actor often used this body language in his movie roles.) Again, the lack of balance and ability to control the body's motion make the individual appear

to be a better target for attack.

Molloy's work also indicates that greater upper body motion is associated with lower socio-economic position. When walking, a lower-middle-class man typically lets his shoulders and body roll, his hips swing and his arms hang outward from his torso. In contrast, body posture for an upper middle-class man included straight shoulders, arms in toward torso and a walk that was almost military. Whether it's their posture or their position, upper-middle-class people are perceived as having more power and authority than those from lower classes. This perception is likely to deter an attacker, so by all means develop an upper-middle class posture.

Overall, your posture and body movement tell a great deal about who you are. From a simple medical point of view, improving the way you hold and move your body will bring better health, greater physical attractiveness and a higher level of emotional well being. Good posture combats stress and fatigue both physically and emotionally. Physically, proper posture provides better alignment of bones and muscle tissue so your body can economize on energy. Emotionally, your posture affects your mood and your mood affects your body. Methods such as Alexander Technique, Feldenkrais Awareness through Movement, and Pilates (see Health, Jan./Feb. 1997 for brief descriptions) can help you develop better posture and change your body language.

Psychology

Facial expressions, posture and body language are all part of the nonverbal communication that goes on continuously between humans. Nelson points out that "nonverbal behaviors account for approximately 65 percent of communication". B. M. DePaulo (Psychological Bulletin, 1992) found that these signals are difficult to hide and can be easily observed by others. For this reason, it's particularly important to develop a strong sense of self esteem, awareness and suspicion as a foundation for your nonverbal communication.

On the other hand, because nonverbal behavior is relatively obvious, it is a tool that you can use in order to avoid problems. For example, in 1988 Ekman, Friesen & O'Sullivan (Journal of Personality and Social Psychology) found that lying with a smile is hard to do. People use more eye muscle movement when they smile truthfully than when they are being deceitful. DePaulo (Journal of Applied Social Psychology, 1989) also found that observers, using nonverbal cues, can tell when a salesperson is lying.

However, in addition to observing you, a potential attacker will often "test" you through both eye contact (see Chapter 9) and physical contact. It's wise to quickly create a safe distance between yourself and anyone who tries to intimidate you by staring. If you show submissiveness by looking down or to the side, you may find yourself mugged. Be particularly suspicious of bumping or shoving. These actions, sometimes with an apology, are often used as a cover up while you are being robbed. Also, try to maintain at least your own body height as your "personal space" between you and suspicious behavior. (Remember, suspicious behavior can come from intimate family and friends or from business associates as well as from strangers. Stress, drugs, alcohol, familiarity, miscommunication, can all trigger behavior that is inappropriate and/or violent.)

Personal space is an egg-shaped area around an individual (larger in the front than on the sides or back) that varies in size depending on your culture and comfort with the other person. According to Edward Hall (The Hidden Dimension, 1966) people use their personal space to communicate with others. Aggressors, for example, may try to crowd you.

For self defense, it's wise to cultivate a personal space that is at least 2 arms lengths or your own body height. Martial arts research shows that when you face another person, your body will automatically twitch as that person crosses the boundary of your personal space. This edge or boundary of the personal space is referred to as the flight/fight zone. When suspicious behavior

occurs outside your personal space, your typical response is to escape (flight). When a problem occurs
inside your personal space, your instinctual response is
to fight. Being conscious of your personal space will
help you judge how to respond to a potential problem.

Nelson suggests several ways that you can use
your own body language to de-escalate a potential problem, including:

- Keep your expression as neutral, calm and atten-
tive as possible to reduce hostility.
- Maintain an alert posture with feet shoulder-width
apart and weight evenly distributed between your feet.
- Keep you body motion to a minimum. Stand still
(don't shift from one foot to the other) and keep your
hands and arms close to your body (avoid large ges-
tures that can be misinterpreted as insults).
- Stay outside the fight/flight zone. This way you
are out of reach if the problem person tries to grab or hit
you.
- Turn your shoulder toward the potential attacker.
By angling your body, you present the hard, bony part
of your torso to the attacker, and protect the more vulnerable areas of yourself from contact. This also puts
you in a position to turn and escape. Be sure to keep
your head turned toward the suspicious person, how-

ever, so you can see what they are doing.

- Keep your hands free and in front of your body so you can use them to block or strike if necessary. Don't cross your arms or shove your hands in your pockets. These can be interpreted as threatening behavior.
- Breath deeply and slowly.

By paying attention to your own nonverbal behavior or body language as well as to that of others, you'll find life more interesting and a lot safer.

Chapter 14

Name:_____

Question 27

Briefly discuss the role of nonverbal behaviors in victimolgy.

Chapter 14

Name:_____

What is the importance of personal space in self-defense?

Legal Postscript

Introduction

The laws of most states provide for the right to defend yourself and others. They also give police departments and officers certain parallel rights. With these rights there are legal responsibilities regarding the use of "excessive force", "mutual combat", and acts of revenge. These legal responsibilities are described in the **Penal Codes** of each state. Violation of these **codes** can lead to arrest and criminal prosecution which can result in a jail term or fine.

Even if your actions are within legal boundaries, you should also consider the risk of civil action (i.e., torts) against you. For example, if you are involved in an altercation, the attacker can actually sue you. If he or she should win, you could lose a lot of money. At the same time it is dangerous to rely solely on police protection because there is a chronic shortage of police personnel in many of our cities. Furthermore many crimes happen so quickly that self-defense is critical for survival. This postscript chapter will give a brief overview of these topics.

Rights And Responsibilities Of Self-Defense

Both legislative actions and superior/supreme court decisions give us the right to defend our life and limb. We also have the right to defend the lives of others. However, legally we are to use only "reasonable force" for our defense.

Reasonable, here, refers to the level of force that "reasonable" people under the same circumstances would use to stop the aggressor(s). What exactly is meant by reasonable force and reasonable people is not always clear. But essentially this means that we are legally obligated to avoid using excessive force to stop the imminent threat to life and limb. Excessive force basically means either too much force given the situation or retaliatory type of force. An example of too much force is the case of the intended rape victim who already had incapacitated the assailant by fracturing his pelvic ring. After he was semi-conscious on the floor and was no longer an immediate threat to her, she continued her counter-attack causing him grievous bodily injury requiring 6 weeks of hospital care. She was arrested and later he sued her. The arrest led to trial. She was lucky to end up with a sympathetic jury which acquitted her of the criminal charges. However, at this writing the attacker's civil suit is still in progress, and it has already cost her several thousand dollars to defend herself.

An example of retaliatory type of force involves the rape victim who, after her ordeal, called the police and identified the attacker. The officers refused to arrest the man because of insufficient "visible" evidence. After the police left, the victim took a loaded shotgun to the man's apartment and shot him. She was arrested by the police and later sued by the rapist in civil court. At this writing no outcome is known yet.

In most jurisdictions "mutual combat" and dueling (pre-arranged combat with deadly weapons) is illegal and punishable by fines and jail terms. If there are no provable signs that you tried to do everything you could to avoid a confrontation with an assailant, your defense may look like mutual combat. We recommend, there-fore, that first and foremost, you try to avoid dangerous situations. If avoidance is impossible try to have wit-nesses who will testify that the attacker forced the de-fensive situation upon you. This, of course, takes some strategy and planning.

An example of good strategy was exercised by a San Francisco martial artist when she was attacked by an-other motorist.* A minor traffic accident (no injuries or

*This account was given to us by the late John Pereira

damage) in busy downtown San Francisco led the victim and the attacker to get out of their vehicles, presumably to look at the damage and to exchange license numbers. The attacker, a rather large and belligerent man, jumped out of his car, and while yelling obscenities and threats moved toward the victim in a threatening way. She, being a trained martial artist, immediately began to retreat around her car giving him plenty of time to change his mind about attacking her. At the same time she was giving the eyewitnesses time to accumulate and to absorb what was happening. He continued to pursue her and moved close enough to hurt her. At this point she defended herself and broke his nose. The police interviewed the witnesses as well as the "combatants" and arrested him. At this writing he did not file a civil lawsuit against her.

A high-ranking New York martial artist was almost the victim of mistaken identity when a man armed with a knife moved toward him while threatening to kill him. The martial artist backed away into the community center building where he was scheduled to teach a self-defense class. Once he was surrounded by eyewitnesses, the armed man ran away.

Civil Suits

In this country anyone can sue anybody for anything.

Underlying this very broad access to the legal system is the philosophy that people don't have to have physical confrontations over disagreements if "impartial" legal processes are available to them.

Unfortunately this means that attackers can use the legal system to harass their victims by filing civil suits against them. Some attackers are so brazen that they file lawsuits against their victims from inside their jail cells. Others sue their victims after they have served their sentence. Furthermore, there are attorneys who are immoral and hungry enough to represent people who file frivolous or unreasonable lawsuits. Also, people can file such lawsuits on their own, even without attorneys.

If you are the target of an unfair lawsuit, your legal recourse is to countersue for malicious use of prosecution. Under certain circumstances such countersuits go after not just the person suing you but also the attorney representing him or her. However, this can cost you more time and money than you might be willing to spend.

A self-employed businessman, for instance, was attacked without provocation by a seemingly deranged man on a Los Angeles street. The intended victim was with his wife and sister-in-law who was visiting from the East Coast. The three were walking from a restaurant to their parked car when a large man assumed a martial arts type of stance and while cursing, lunged toward the victim who had training in karate. The "victim" counterpunched just once, breaking the attacker's jaw and knocking out two of his teeth.

The police interviewed five witnesses and determined that the punch was, under the circumstances, legally justifiable and made no arrests. Later, the attacker sued the victim for medical costs and punitive damages. The victim fought the suit and three years later won. It cost the victim thousands of dollars in legal fees to win his case. Furthermore, the time taken from his business due to deposition hearings, court appearances and lawyer conferences cost him several thousand dollars more. Although the court directed the attacker to reimburse the victim for his losses, the indigent attacker was unable to do so.

In another case, a Chicago martial arts instructor was in the middle of teaching a class when a man came running into the studio and began to repeatedly swing punches at him. By instinct the instructor defended himself by doing a well-practiced, self-defense routine which broke the attacker's nose, left collarbone and two ribs. The attacker sued both the instructor and the studio owner. The attacker lost, but it took the "victims" four years and almost $10,000.00 of direct and indirect costs to legally defend themselves in spite of having nearly 30 students who eyewitnessed the incident.

Unfortunately, these abuses of the justice system are so common that we recommend not fighting unless you have absolutely no choice. However, if you have no alternative, then fight vigorously. Your action may make the difference between life and death. As the old adage says: "I'd rather be judged by 12 than carried by 6."

Police Protection: Fact Or Myth?

According to the FBI's Uniform Crime Reports, violent crimes increased by nearly 45% during a recent 10 year period. During the same time period there was "no significant" change in the size of police departments. In other words, the social environment has become more dangerous for all of us while police departments, for a variety of reasons, have not increased their size at the same rate.

Furthermore, even where "small" law enforcement bodies are impressive, arrests for violent crimes often don't lead to convictions. Extrapolations from a variety of situations, both reported and unreported, suggest that between 60% and 80% of violent crimes in America do not result in convictions. A recent issue of the *Los Angeles Times* newspaper, for instance, reported that in Southern California nearly 70% of homocides are unsolved.

Unfortunately the low rates of arrest and conviction encourage criminal activity. Numerous studies also indicate that it is the likelihood of arrest and conviction, rather than the severity of punishment which deters crime. (See, for example, Silberman's book, **Criminal Violence, Criminal Justice**, chapters 6 through 8.) Thus crime is increasing and neither police presence nor legal action is keeping pace.

In addition, nationwide there are about 600,000 men and women in our jails. And, in the opinion of many judges, many jails are already overcrowded. However, judging from the arrest and conviction rates there may be another approximately 2 million people who should be in jail but are not (about 1% of the U.S. population).

Nationwide there are only about 500,000 active police personnel, leaving many jurisdictions with an extreme shortage of police officers and, therefore, protection. The city of Los Angeles, for example, has a population of about 3.5 to 4.5 million (depending on whether you are counting commuters and temporary residents). But the city has only about 9000 full-time (regular) police officers and about 1000 part-time (reserve) police officers and other volunteers. Police departments, however, are attempting to operate more effectively. For example, departments in many cities, such as Los Angeles, are using a prioritized system of response which classifies police department calls into three groups.

The highest level call includes life-and-death emergencies such as robberies in progress, rapes in progress, shots being fired, and so on. Under the prioritized system, every area (i.e., Division or Precinct) has a small number of two-officer black-and-white cars (Adam units) to respond to these urgent cases. Helicopters often provide additional help to these emergency police cars. In Los Angeles, the response time to emergency calls is about 2-7 minutes which compares favorably with the national average of about 15 minutes.

A police department using a prioritized system of response typically has several one-officer black-and-whites (L-Cars) which are available to back up the Adam units or to respond to the lower than life-and-death priority calls. These less critical calls include, for instance, burglary calls in which the burglar has left the scene. Or perhaps there's a loud party without any known danger. The response time for these less dangerous calls can be quite long, sometimes two or more hours.

The third level of response is to calls involving no danger. A one-person report car (LAPD's U-car or G-car), for example, might be used to take a residential burglary report where the victim has returned from a vacation to find his residence burglarized and has already established that there is no burglar inside. These calls can have very long response times—sometimes even 24 hours.

Even though the prioritized system helps to speed response times to emergency calls, the slower police response times to non-emergency calls very often arouse the anger of the victims who, at times, unjustly accuse the police officers or the department of not doing their job. The relatively small size of the police department also necessitates many calls being taken by phone without police appearance on the scene. Most vandalism reports as well as thefts/burglaries from motor vehicles are taken over the phone. This, too, makes many angry at the police. For example, one irate citizen complained "...but it's MY Porche that was vandalized, and I want a fingerprinting team here, NOW!"

Sometimes citizens displace their anger onto the responding officers and insist on filing formal complaints against them. All of these complaints are investigated, and this takes time which further lessens police presence in the streets.

Even when the response time is under two minutes, you are at risk. Some rapists complete their assault in less than two minutes. With weapons you can be murdered or maimed within seconds. In summary, police protection is not perfect. We therefore recommend that you be alert, aware and prepared so that you can avoid criminal violence. Use self-defense skills only if you must, because even self-defense has risks both physically and legally.

The vast majority of Americans in all neighborhoods across the country are law abiding. They don't burglarize, they don't attack each other and they don't commit murder. We are referring, here, to the 99% of Americans who receive the tiny fraction of the media coverage given to bizarre murderers, rapists, looters, rioters, drug dealers, etc.

These law abiding people are, nevertheless, concerned about being victimized and unprotected as they go about their legal business. This concern combined with their ubiquity places them in a good position to cooperate with their local police department in a variety of ways to reduce violent crime.

Many police departments have a variety of programs designed to control crime by way of police-citizen cooperation. The Los Angeles Police Department has, for instance, the **Lady Beware** presentations (anti-rape), the **D.A.R.E.** program (anti-drug), **Crime Prevention** workshops (anti-burglary/battery), **Neighborhood Watch**, and the **Reserve Officer Corps** (unpaid, part-time police officers).

Local police working in cooperation with the law abiding members of their community may be what is needed to reverse the epidemic of violent crime in the U.S.

CHAPTER 16

Conclusion

For survival and success, we encourage you to learn to prevent problems, to avoid danger, and to fight when necessary.

Prevent Problems

A strong sense of self respect will help you recognize danger and give you the opportunity to prevent problems. Anyone who tries to intrude on you physically or emotionally is violating your rights. Don't pick up hitchhikers or allow strangers into your home. When answering strangers, be cool and businesslike. Keep at least two arms' length of space between you and a stranger so he or she can't grab you.

Choose activities in your life that help you develop independence and the ability to cope. You can look for growth opportunities at work or at school that stretch your abilities. Also select hobbies and recreational activities to expand your experience and physical skill. You might also find family responsibilities and home projects that challenge you and build your confidence and self esteem.

Develop a willingness to fight back. A simple self-defense course will increase your ability to sense danger by recognizing when your space is being invaded. It will teach when and why to be "rude" and refuse requests for help. It will also teach you how to strike back, yell and gouge. And it will help you feel comfortable using these "aggressive" but effective techniques!

Avoid Danger

As we've pointed out throughout this book, you should avoid offering opportunities to strangers—they might turn into attackers. For example, if you receive unwanted phone calls, simply hang up. Avoid walking alone at night. If you see someone following you, change directions.

Don't be afraid to run away from a dangerous situation. Escaping or fleeing is one of the most successful ways to avoid an attack or rape.

Also, learn to react as soon as possible. Often assailants count on surprising their victims. By responding quickly, you can catch an attacker unaware, giving yourself the chance to run, yell or fight.

Fight When Necessary

Research shows that physical resistance stops attackers, and the sooner and more vigorously you respond, the more successful you will be. Learning to fight will increase your ability to resist successfully. Also expect to use more than one form of resistance regardless of how well trained you are as a fighter. Dr. Bart found that women who avoided rape when confronted usually used at least three strategies. Strategies included getting help from an outsider (successful 83% of the time) fleeing (successful 81% of the time), fighting (68% success rate), yelling (63% success) and reasoning (54% success rate).

By developing your awareness and ability in terms of prevention, avoidance and fighting skill, you'll gain a stronger sense of your personal value and your right to be alive, unharmed and happy.

Bibliography

Abel, G.G., Barlow, D.H., Blanchard, E.B., and Guild, D. The components of rapists' sexual arousal. Paper presented at the American Psychiatric Asssociation meeting, May 1975, Anaheim, California.

Amir, M. **Patterns of Forcible Rape**. Chicago: University of Chicago Press, 1971.

Anderson, K. Fight Exercise Boredom With A Martial Art. *Executive Fitness*. 1989, August: 4-5.

Bart, P.B., and O'Brien, P.H. **Stopping Rape: Successful Survival Strategies**. New York: Pergamon Press, 1988.

Barthol, R.G. **Protect Yourself**. Englewood Cliffs, New Jersey: Prentice-Hall, 1979.

Brownmiller, S. **Against Our Will: Men, Women and Rape**. New York: Simon & Schuster, 1975.

Burgess, A.W., and Holmstrom, L.L. The Rape Victim in the Emergency Ward. *American Journal of Nursing*. Oct. (1973): 1740- 45.

Butterer, K. Getting Straight. *Health*, Jan./Feb. (1997): 84.

Caignon, D., and Groves, G. **Her Wits About Her: Self-Defense Success Stories by Women**. New York: Harper & Row, 1987.

Cohen, M., and Seghorn, T. Sociometric Study of the Sex Offender. *J. Abnormal Psych.* 1969, 74, 249-255.

Coleman, J.C., Butcher, J.N., and Carson, R.C. Abnormal Psychology and Modern Life (3rd ed.). Glenview, Ill.: Scott, Foresman and Company, 1984.

Cratty, B.J. Psychology in Contemporary Sport. Englewood Cliffs, N.J.: Prentice-Hall, 1973.

Cuevas, C., Danowski, K., Giggans, P., and Ledley, E. Surviving Domestic Violence: A safety & empowering guide for battered women. Los Angeles: L.A. Commission On Assaults Against Women, 1989.

DePaulo, B. M. Nonverbal Behavior and Self Presentation. *Psychological Bulletin*, 1992, 111: 203-243.

DePaulo, P.J., & DePaulo, B.M. Can Deception by Salespersons and Customers be Detected Through Nonverbal Behavioral Cues? *Journal of Applied Social Psychology*, 1989, 19: 1552-1577.

Ekman, P, Friesen, W.V. & O'Sullivan, M. Smiles When Lying. *Journal of Personality and Social Psychology*, 1988, 54: 414-420.

Feshbach, S., and Feshbach, N. The Young Aggressors. *Psychology Today*, 1973, 6: 90-95.

Festinger, L. A Theory of Cognitive Dissonance. Stanford, Calif.: Stanford University Press, 1957.

Fox, J.R. Inhibition, Aggression, and Kinship. Paper presented at a seminar, Recent Studies Concerning

Dominance, Aggression, and Violence. New York: Rockefeller University, 1983, January 18.

Gates, D. **Standards and Procedures Regarding Domestic Violence.** Los Angeles Police Department. **Memorandum No. 1.** 1986, February.

Grayson, B. A Comparison of Criminal Perceptions of the Nonverbal Behavior of Potential Victims of Assault & a Movement Analysis Based on Lab Analysis. *Dissertation*, State University of New York at Albany, 1978.

Hall, E.T. **The Hidden Dimension,** Garden City, NY: Doubleday, 1966.

Herrington, L. **Preface** to the Final Report. **U.S. Attorney's Report on Family Violence.** Washington: Department of Justice. 1984.

Hilgard, E.R., Atkinson, R.L., and Atkinson, R.C. **Introduction to Psychology** (7th Ed.). New York: Harcourt, Brace, Jovanovich, 1979.

Johnson, J. Ninja Hero or Master Fake? **Valley Sec**tion of the *Los Angeles Times*. 1988, May 1: 4-11.

Kirsch, J. Los Angeles Police Dept. Consultant, 1994.

Latane, B., and Darley, J.M. **The Unresponsive Bystander: Why Doen't He Help?** New York: Appleton-Century-Crofts, 1970.

Lawther, J.D. **Sport Psychology.** Englewood Cliffs, N.J.: Prentice- Hall, 1972.

London, P. Beginning Psychology. Homewood, Ill.: The Dorsey Press, 1979.

Maccoby, E.E., and Jacklin, C.N. The Psychology of Sex Differences. Stanford, Calif.: Stanford Univ. Press, 1974.

Maslow, A.H. Motivation and Personality. New York: Harper and Row, 1954.

McCormick, E.J., and Tiffin, J. Industrial Psychology (6th Ed.). Englewood Cliffs, N.J.: Prentice-Hall, 1974.

Medea, A., and Thompson, K. Against Rape. New York: Farrar, Straus and Giroux, 1974.

Metzler,B. Abuse, Neglect of Dependent Elders Emerges as New "National Pastime." Part I of the Los Angeles Times. 1989, August 20: 11.

Molloy, J. T. Molloy's Live for Success. New York: Bantam Books, 1981.

National Coalition Against Domestic Violence. NCADV Statistics Pamphlet. 1990. Washington, D.C.

National Coalition Against Domestic Violence. On Verbal/Emotional Abuse... Pamphlet. 1989. Washington, D.C.

National Coalition Against Domestic Violence. What Is Battering/Who Is Battered? Pamphlet. 1988. Washington, D.C.

National Coalition Against Domestic Violence. Power and Control Pamphlet. 1988. Washington. D.C.

Nelson, J. Self Defense, Steps to Success. 1991.

Offir, C.W. Psychology Today. January, 1975.

Paffenbarger, R. Untitled article in *Executive Fitness Newsletter*, January, 1978.

Peachy, R. National Estimates & Facts About Domestic Violence. A fact sheet distributed by the Southern California Coalition On Battered Women. Santa Monica, California. 1989.

Puskas, F., and Weiss, B.W.. Psychology and Methods of Survival. Los Angeles: Hiles & Hardin, 1986.

Queen's Bench Foundation's Project Rape Response, *U.S. Dept. of Justice*, 1976.

Rada, R.T. Clinical Aspects of the Rapist. New York: Grune and Stratton, 1978.

Revitch, E., and Weiss, R.G. The Pedophiliac Offender. *Dis. Nerv. Sys.*, 1962, 23, 73-78.

Selkin, J. Rape: When to Fight Back. *Psychology Today*. January, 1975.

Silberman, C.E. Criminal Violence, Criminal Justice. New York: Vintage Books. 1980.

Sgroi, S.M. Sexual Molestation of Children: The Last Frontier in Child Abuse. In S. Chess & A. Thomas (Eds.)., Annual Progress In Child Psychiatry and Child Development. New York: Brunner/Mazel. 1976.

Smith, M. Smoke From An Urbane Volcano. *Sports Illustrated.* 1975: 28-31.

Sports Psychology. August 18, 1975.

Stransky, Judith & Stone, Robert B. The Alexander Technique: Joy in the Life of Your Body. New York: Beaufort Books, 1981.

Swanson, D.W. Adult Sexual Abuse of Children: The Man and Circumstance. *Dis. Nerv. Sys.* 1968, 29, 677-683.

Take a Stand! *Mademoiselle*, December 1996: 102

Titley, R.W., and Viney, W. Expression of Aggression Toward the Physically Handicapped. *Perceptual and Motor Skills*, 1969, 29: 51-56.

Warshaw, R. Should You Fight Back Against A Criminal? *Woman's Day.* 1989, August 15: 34-38.

Weiss, B.W. **Woman As Victim.** Los Angeles: Werner/Michael, 1977.

Weiss, B.W. Legal Side: Martial Arts, the Law and You. *Bugeisha.* 1997-Pres. A regular column.

Weiss, B.W. **Self-Defense in Traditional Kata, Volumes I through XII.** Los Angeles: Hiles & Hardin, Beginning with 1999 through (est.) 2004.

Weiss, B.W., *et al.* The Destructive Impact of Karate Punches vs 9mm Ammunition Through Body Armor. **KSI Report 303.** Los Angeles: Ken Studies Institute, 1995.

Weiss, B.W., and Weiss, H.O. **Urban Survival: Applied Psychology and Methods.** Los Angeles: Hiles & Hardin, 1995.

Weiss, B.W., and Weiss, H.O. **Self-Defense For**

Everybody: A Primer in Applied Karate. Los Angeles: Hiles & Hardin, 1992.

West's California Codes. Penal Code of California. St. Paul: Minn.: West Publishing Co. 1999.

Yonce, E.L. **Lady Beware** of Sexual Assault. Unpublished paper at the Los Angeles Police Department's West Valley Area Community Relations Office.

Index

A